NATIONAL
STRATEGY INFORMATION CENTER, INC.

D0888127

OIL, DIVESTITURE AND NATIONAL SECURITY

M. A. Adelman · William J. Casey
Edward W. Erickson · Marshall I. Goldman
William A. Johnson · Klaus Knorr
Richard E. Messick

AND SELECTED CONGRESSIONAL TESTIMONY

PREFACE BY
Frank R. Barnett

EDITOR
Frank N. Trager

PUBLISHED BY
CRANE, RUSSAK & COMPANY, INC.
NEW YORK

Oil, Divestiture and National Security

Published by
Crane, Russak & Company, Inc.
347 Madison Avenue
New York, N.Y. 10017

ISBN 0-8448-1070-3
LC 76-51876

Printed in the United States of America

Table of Contents

Preface

Some readers may wonder why a Center normally concerned with questions of strategy and geopolitics should address itself to the dispute over divestiture of US oil corporations, which seems to pit consumer interests against profits. One can imagine a critic asking: "Isn't the proposal to bust up Big Oil, in the name of competition and social justice, a *domestic economic* issue? If so, is there really anything relevant to be said by people whose focus is on international security affairs? Why not let consumer advocates and big businessmen slug it out on their own turf?" For a number of reasons, we conclude that, as in most things human, the issue is not as simplistic as indignant slogan-eers would have us believe. In fact, analysis suggests that framing the debate as "consumerism *vs.* oligopoly" is a form of misleading polemics, obscuring the awesome implications of divestiture for foreign policy and national defense.

The question of US security has been largely ignored by advocates of divestiture, except for those who advance the curious hypothesis that, since giant corporations are too pliable in Arab hands, breaking them into smaller units would somehow liberate American foreign policy from the same pressures. Does this mean that if Saudi Arabia with 28 percent of the world's oil reserves, can face down Aramco, the Saudis would somehow be overawed by a pack of "mom and pop" wildcatters? Or does it imply that—in the event of another embargo—Washington would be more likely to dispatch warships to the Persian

Gulf in support of a host of mini-companies in their resistance to OPEC? Is it postulated that small-time operators with modest cash flow would be less difficult for the Arabs to manipulate and "whip-saw" than the large MNCs with their huge capital reserves, global options, and staying power? To pose the questions is to dispose of the premise. To prescribe shattering the structure and dispersing the professional management of big-league American oil companies as a means to "overcome" the OPEC challenge is rather like arguing that fragmenting the Pentagon is the best way to "intimidate" the Soviet military.

Is it not self-evident that OPEC's pricing and Arab embargo policies are driven by factors other than the size and combined functions of American oil companies? The Shah of Iran's well-known desire for higher oil prices stems from the enormous cost of his country's internal development program and a feeling that, unless the promises of the "white" revolution are met, a revolution of a darker color will ensue. With regard to embargos, Washington's resolve either to sell or with-hold sophisticated weaponry to particular states in the Middle East must surely have greater significance for Arab decisionmakers than the expected results of divestiture.

Making an immediate command decision to invest $25 billion, at minimum, in searching out new oil reservoirs, upgrading recovery technology, liquifying and gasifying coal, and putting solar energy satellites into space would also underscore our serious intent to weaken the existing cartel. Given the lead-time factor, it will be difficult to escape dependence on OPEC over the next decade. Beyond that, real options exist, most of them involving enormous capital outlays and the sort of large-scale technology that only giant corporations can mar-shal; but those who prefer to exorcise the hoary specter of "malefactors of great wealth" seem not greatly attached to such pragmatic solutions.

Another tack employed by some proponents of divestiture is to argue that OPEC is a scarecrow, energy shortage is a convenient fiction, and control over US *domestic* production, transportation, refining, and marketing is the lever by which American oil companies manipulate prices. If this theory were true, one would be hard put to explain the even higher prices of gasoline in foreign areas not served by American oil companies, except by postulating an even wider "conspiracy" in-volving Socialist and even Communist governments as secret partners of our MNCs. In fact, a striking paradox reveals itself in pro-divestiture polemics; that is, a "progressive" label is attached to parochial prejudices against "internationalism," and the "liberal" prescription for dealing with the modern web of complex joint ventures is the formula of the Luddites.

Perhaps it must be said one more time: The energy shortage is real. It is persistent. We will never get back to "normalcy" as we defined that term in the Summer of 1973. The era of cheap oil, like the era of cheap domestic servants, is past and gone, but not because oil companies are conspiring against the consumer (although some businessmen, like some politicians and some labor leaders, may on occasion put personal advantage above the public interest). In this instance, the "conspiracy" evolves from tens of millions of new babies each year and the ambition of their parents (all colors, all races) who "plot" to substitute machine power for human muscle. For we no longer live in a segregated world in which Americans drive cars, Europeans ride bicycles, and Asians plod behind their water buffalo. On all continents, including the poorest quarters of Asia, Africa, and Latin America, trucks and Hondas, factories and tractors, irrigation pumps and petrochemical plants are drinking oil. And with every year that passes, as population grows and development spreads, simply "keeping even" will accelerate the rate of global oil depletion. The energy crisis is pervasive; it won't go away; it affects all mankind; and it won't be solved by the artificial and irrelevant truncation of American corporations.

There is another point that needs reiteration. However comforting it may be to believe that Project Independence, if resolutely executed, would speedily free the United States from dependence on Middle East sources of oil, the facts are at variance with the hope. In spite of "independence" rhetoric, we rely even more on Persian Gulf sources today than we did before the Arab boycott. A few statistics illustrate the reason why. While the United States has some six percent of proven world oil reserves, the Persian Gulf region holds nearly 66 percent. Consuming six billion barrels per year, an America relying exclusively on its own proven reserves, including the new potential of Alaska, would exhaust these completely in not more than seven years. According to the Federal Energy Administration, by 1980 we will need to import over 50 percent of our oil requirements. Based on current free world reserves and rates of production, the bulk of the increase in imported oil will have to come from Arab members of OPEC. Western Hemisphere supplies, including Canada and Venezuela, are diminishing; and, while the flow from Nigeria has increased temporarily, in the medium and long run we will necessarily become ever more dependent upon Saudi Arabia. All of which is to emphasize that the geology and politics of the Middle East, plus the naval balance of the superpowers in the Indian Ocean/Persian Gulf theater, will be infinitely more relevant to our future energy problems than the shape and number of American oil companies.

Inasmuch as the energy crisis is global, and since national security as well as "economic" questions are involved, it may prove useful to rethink the hypothesis that large US corporations should be further curtailed in the public interest. Owing to our antitrust legislation—and an adversary relationship between many government agencies and private business—American enterprise is already more regulated and more competitive than most of its opposite numbers elsewhere (Japan, France, Germany, for a start). If we have less than a perfect free market, at least we have competition among 20 major oil companies, far more than any other country. Even though there are joint ventures, these arrangements by no means constitute a "cartel" in the European or Japanese sense, let alone the sort of monopoly power over resources exercised by the governments and pseudocorporations of the Socialist bloc. There is little point in pretending that other nations are likely to impose divestiture on their own consortiums and state-subsidized conglomerates in order to promote competition and consumerism. In the continuing scramble for scarce resources—a contest that will become even more intense in the 1980s—the national purpose may best be served by American corporations large enough to provide the global logistics, buffer stocks, and financial reserves required in what may yet evolve into a "resource war." In dealing with the state cartels of Iran, Saudi Arabia, Iraq, and Kuwait, or in possible competition with Japan, Inc., do we really want to field lightweight teams for the world energy cup match? Professor Goldman, in Chapter Five of this book, makes the further point in terms of our most persistent adversary:

> What is a paradox, however, is that while we seem to be contemplating steps which could well reduce our overall competitive-

ness in world petroleum markets, the Soviet Union is doing exactly the opposite—and, indeed, is vigorously improving its economic positions by building up its own integrated international petroleum corporations.

A recent story in the *New York Times* further illustrates the "conflict" facet of the energy problem in a manner that suggests the advantage, in a highly competitive world, of having large-scale and thoroughly professional oil companies on our side. The *Times* story (September 17, 1976) describes a multinational exercise to simulate another oil embargo and test plans to share oil in an emergency among 19 industrial nations. Involving more than 30 oil companies, the exercise was directed from the International Energy Agency in Paris, an entity created as a result of the 1973-74 Arab embargo on oil shipments to the United States and the Netherlands. The national defense nuances of the test were indicated by the remark of a planner with one of the American companies: "Don't use the word war-games, but it's probably the most descriptive word."

If and when we are confronted with another embargo, imposed by Arab state cartels to alter or undermine the goals of US foreign policy, the management expertise of our large oil companies will be a critical national security asset, as the following paragraphs of the *Times* story make clear.

> Among the 19 international energy agency members are the United States, Canada, Britain, France, West Germany, and Japan.

> The United States took the lead in forging this alliance of oil-consuming countries to devise new ways to conserve energy, to collaborate in development of new energy sources, to show the oil-exporting states that the importers would help each other in time of need, and to strengthen Washington's position as a global leader.

> The view in Washington and in other capitals is that if another shortage occurs, the oil companies will have to carry the burden of managing supplies, as they did in 1973-74. The companies have done most of the planning, under federal and international supervision.

An American oil executive made the same point, saying of the October-November test: "The companies will probably do 99 percent of the job, as they did in the last crisis. As we look at it, this is just formalization of what we had before."

The more usual, "domestic" rationale for divestiture is often expressed as follows: (1) energy, as imperative to our well-being as water and air, is arbitrarily controlled by a handful of giant firms whose sole aim is to maximize profits; (2) breaking up the 20 largest oil companies will restore competition, reduce costs, and benefit the consumer. Therefore (it is argued), by means of legislation to enforce *vertical* divestiture, a large firm should no longer be permitted to explore-produce, transport, refine, and market its own oil, but should engage in only one of those activities; and further, via legislation to ensure *horizontal* divestiture, an oil company over a certain size should not be permitted to invest in other energy enterprises such as coal, oil shale, uranium, coal gasification, solar, and geothermal.

These questions—relating to operating costs, competition, efficiency, and capital risk—are explored in the following chapters by authorities from different disciplines. Moreover, the domestic side of the problem is placed in its proper international setting, as we seek in the immediate future, and for much of the next two decades, to improve our deteriorating energy posture. The diverse perspectives of the authors of this book will provide the thoughtful reader with a multifaceted picture of the divestiture issue—which must be evaluated in *all* of its important dimensions, including that of defense and security.

Frank R. Barnett, *President*
National Strategy Information Center, Inc.

December 1976

1

The Changing Structure of
Big International Oil

M. A. ADELMAN

A look backward is essential to understand the present.[1] Before
World War II, producers of crude oil outside the United States were
few in number because entry into the field was very costly and risky.
There were relatively few refiners as well, but for a different reason.
Refined-product markets were small and closed off to competition from
outside a given country. Refiners disliked buying from the few sellers
of crude oil, and the sellers did not like to sell to the few buyers.
Hence, there was a good reason why refiners "had to" own their own
crude, and why producers "had to" have their own refineries. And as
they integrated forward from production or backward from refining,
they forced any other entrant to do likewise, and thus precluded an
open market in crude oil. In this way, a concentrated, integrated market
structure perpetuated itself.

The few integrated firms restrained competition, and during 1928-39
they operated a cartel. After World War II, this cartel was never
revived—legend to the contrary notwithstanding. But the world market
(then excluding the United States, the Communist countries, and some
small nations) was the preserve of eight large oil companies. In 1950,
Exxon, BP, Shell, and Gulf produced 83 percent of the crude oil in

---

[1] The following four paragraphs are based on my book, *The World Petroleum Market* (Baltimore: Johns Hopkins University Press for Resources For The Future, 1972).

this market; while Texaco, Standard of California, Mobil, and CFP produced the rest. By 1969, the biggest four were down to 64 percent, and the big eight a total of 81 percent. The companies scrupulously avoided any collusion ("the New England conscience is deeply rooted in fear of the police"); but the fact that they participated in a number of joint ventures, especially in the Persian Gulf, enabled each of them to know a good deal about the short- and long-run plans of its rivals.

The degree of vertical integration also diminished slowly during those years. In 1950, about seven percent of the crude oil in the world market was sold at arms' length; and by 1970, the total was about 21 percent. But barriers to entry were still very great because refineries were mostly owned by producers of very low-cost—hence very profitable—crude. Even so, this very slow growth of competition had a powerful effect on prices. Between 1947 and early 1970, the "real" or constant-dollar crude oil price at the Persian Gulf, decreased by approximately 65 percent. The multinational companies deserve neither credit nor blame. They competed only as much as the market structure compelled them to, but it compelled a good deal. During these years, billions of dollars flowed into the world industry; rather than a shortage of investment, there was a chronic potential surplus of oil.

The competitive erosion of price was a challenge; and the response was the creation of the greatest monopoly of all time. From late 1970, the long evolution was triumphantly reversed. Persian Gulf prices sextupled in real terms, that is, from about $1.30 to $11.50, while the general price level rose by about 40 percent.[2] The reason, as everyone knows, was the emergence of the cartel of the OPEC countries (not OPEC itself, which is of very limited importance). Throughout, the United States government helped. In 1970, when Libyan demands promised to blow the door open, some companies thought capitulation even more dangerous than resistance. Some disagreed, some others waffled. But the US government had its way, which was to give the Libyans what they wanted. Thus encouraged, the Persian Gulf countries made their demands in early 1971, and again the public record is clear that our government was more than helpful, and hopeful. The State Department called a special conference to announce that it "expected the previously turbulent international oil situation to calm

---

2 The 1970 price for Arabian 34°; see fn. 1. The $11.50 is the official price as of January 1, 1976. The US GNP deflator is taken as the general price level.

down following the new agreement," and it naturally wanted the credit for the new order.[3]

During 1971-73, the OPEC nations raised the price of crude oil through a charade of "negotiations" with the oil companies, and then the imposition of a unilateral raise in 1973, just before the unexpected Yom Kippur War. The price explosion at the end of 1973 accomplished quickly what would otherwise have happened slowly, step by step. From about $8.00 per barrel at the start of 1974 (disregarding some lunatic prices, and looking at arrangements as they were then, not as retroactively changed) the price was raised to $10.46. In 1974, Saudi Arabia repeatedly claimed to be bringing prices down, and was applauded by the United States, only to take the lead in raising prices.[4] The 1975 increase to $11.50 was part of the monopolists' learning process of finding out how far they could raise the price beyond the range of what was previously known. The companies were expropriated in fact, and largely—but not completely—in law.

The Oil Cartel: How It Works

The oil cartel is a complex phenomenon, but its pricing objectives and operations are simple economics. The political aspects are minor, if not negligible. The oil-producing nations have widely disparate political interests. Some 40 percent of cartel production is non-Arab; and even among the Arabs, there are important dissensions. But there is no opposition between economic and political goals, and consequently no need to sacrifice one for the other. Money is power. The richer these governments, the greater their political weight.

But the cartel as a price-fixing exercise is much stronger because its members are sovereign states. First, cartel governments can use military force to suppress competition. If the production share available to Saudi Arabia is not satisfactory (see below for reasons), they will soon be able to invade and occupy the small sheikdoms of the southern Persian Gulf. Local population is scanty, armaments small, the terrain ideal for a quick move. The United States is sending the Saudis the arms. Doubtless Iran will insist on its share of the booty,

3 Letter, Sir David Barran to Senator Frank Church, in *Multinational Oil Companies and US Foreign Policy, Hearings before the Subcommittee on Multinational Corporations of the Committee on Foreign Relations,* US Senate, 93rd Congress, 2nd Session, Part 8, pages 771-773. See also Anthony Sampson, *The Seven Sisters, The Great Oil Companies and the World They Shaped* (New York: Viking, 1975), pp. 211-215. Mr. Sampson's competence as a journalist-observer has not been questioned.

4 There is no published series of actual contemporary rather than retrospective prices. For the comic sequence of 1974, see the *New York Times,* June 9, June 11, October 13, 1974; *Oil and Gas Journal,* October 21, December 23, 1974.

especially since they can close the exit from the Persian Gulf. The knowledge of this backstop or safety net is an important element of cartel strength.

The cartel is also fortunate in that it need fear no dirty tricks from the customers. Most cartels lead a nervous, harassed life, always looking out for the countermoves of buyers who try to induce lower prices by offering incremental business. But the consuming nations (aside from the occasional empty bluster of the United States) have from the first avoided any resistance, for reasons which future historians may make clear.[5] Their cooperative policies may be good or bad for other reasons. They are an important element of cartel strength.

The experience of the socalled "embargo" was part of the cartel's learning process. There was, in fact, no embargo. There was a production cutback and an exchange of customers. Arab oil went to non-US customers, non-Arab oil to the United States, and everyone suffered about the same degree of import reduction—the "friendly" British, the "odiously neutral" Japanese, and the "unfriendly" United States. As for the companies, they acted wisely to anticipate the inevitable. Without them, oil would have been equalized after prices rose in the "embargoed" countries, and non-Arab governments did good by doing well out of the localized scarcities.[6] The mile-long gasoline lines in the United States were the obvious result of price controls, with no attempt to tax or ration in order to restrain demand. The chaos was made in the USA, not in Arabia.

Throughout this affair, the United States was concerned above all not to offend Saudi Arabia. Our ambassador there privately urged American citizens to pressure our own government to agree to Arab demands;[7] and in November 1973, he publicly predicted "critical" east coast shortages of industrial fuel oil "within days," lest anyone fail to panic.[8] Our government covered up a cut-off of oil supplies to the US Navy from European and Asian refineries, until it was revealed by a business journal.[9]

---

[5] Sampson, *op. cit.*, pp. 216-226; "How OPEC Came to Power," *Forbes*, April 15, 1976, pp. 69-85; Adelman, *op. cit.*, pp. 250-256.

[6] Robert B. Stobaugh, "The Oil Companies in the Crisis," *Daedalus*, Fall 1975, pp. 179-202. The characterizations are from current newspapers.

[7] *Multinational Oil Companies and US Foreign Policy*, p. 513.

[8] *New York Times*, November 10, 1973.

[9] *Ibid.*, January 24, 25, and 26, 1974, referring to proceedings before the US Senate Permanent Subcommittee on Investigations. However, *Business Week* had already reported the fact.

The slogan "cooperation not confrontation" sums up the consuming countries' view of the cartel as a political problem to be solved by negotiation or force. Force is unthinkable. But negotiation or agreement with a group of sovereign monopolists is absurd. A bargain is enforced by competition or law, or both. Anyone who persistently breaks his word finds himself without customers and suppliers, who go elsewhere. Or a court can make him perform. But the monopoly has suppressed competition, so that there is no other place to go. And sovereign states are beyond any law.

The demand for divestiture of the oil companies is merely one additional symptom of the inability of government and public opinion to see an economic problem for what it is.

The Position of Saudi Arabia

In any case, the world structure of big oil is now the structure of the governments as owners and sellers of crude oil in the international market, which today includes the United States. Of the thirteen OPEC nations which now account for the great bulk of world trade, the big four (Saudi Arabia, Iran, Venezuela, and Iraq) now produce 63 percent of the total. The next four largest (Kuwait, Nigeria, UAR, and Libya) account for another 26 percent. Thus, the degree of concentration among the new owners is about where it was among the companies, before the great takeover. But these new owners are unintegrated. They sell practically all their crude oil to the former owners, the resident producing companies.[10] Obviously, disintegration (via expropriation) did not prevent the sextupling of constant-dollar prices.

The producing countries are not a simple monopoly but rather a cartel. Some would argue that although Saudi Arabia has less than 30 percent of the market, it makes all the necessary decisions to restrict supply. That may someday be the case, but not today. If all other countries were permitted to go flat out, and produce to the limit, with Saudi Arabia taking the remainder of the market, then the Saudis would be down to about two or three million barrels daily out of a total (in round numbers) of 30 MBD.[11] The Saudis have made much confident or threatening talk about how they really do not want to produce as much as they do. Sheik Yamani has told us, with-

---

10 The most convenient source of production statistics and company-government arrangements is the monthly *Petroleum Economist* (London).

11 For estimated capacity, see the Federal Energy Administration's *Monthly Energy Review*.

out a smile, that they produce more than suits their economic interest, and this amounts to "losing money," in order to help the world economy.[12] Anyone is free to believe this; some people will believe anything. But Saudi Arabia is now trying to force the local resident company, Aramco, to produce seven MBD. They will tolerate less. Nobody, not even they, knows how far down they can be forced. They hope never to find out.

Anyone trying to make sense of the cartel must begin with a basic equation. World energy demand *less* nonoil supply *less* non-OPEC oil *less* the output of the "fringe" OPEC nations *equals* what is left for Saudi Arabia. I expect that over the next five to ten years, OPEC capacity and production will both continue to grow, and that the excess will stay large.[13] If so, the cartel will remain a cartel and not a single-firm monopoly.

But anyone who looks at the equation can see how a minor mistake early on becomes amplified into a big mistake at the end. Suppose we forecast 65 MBD world consumption in 1980, and it turns out to be really 70 MBD. We would be only seven percent wrong. Yet a difference of five MBD for Saudi Arabia marks the difference between eight MBD and three MBD. If they can have eight MBD, they will be content to let all other governments produce to their limits. If they are left with only three MBD, they will insist on strong restrictions on the production of other countries.

Price Instabilities

But in addition to these uncertainties about total demand and supply, small disturbances can have big results, because this cartel—like all other cartels—is unstable. A cartel is the home of the self-fulfilling prophecy, and the self-reinforcing trend. If various cartel nations believe the cartel will soon come to an end, then it will soon come to an end, as they start producing to the limit.

Conversely, high prices tend to reinforce themselves. High oil prices yield revenues which exceed the commitments of the producing countries. With a surplus, they are willing to restrict output. Were prices lower, they would be forced to sell small additional amounts in order to pay their debts. This can be the ruination of cartels. Sellers know perfectly well that they ought not to try to shove their partners

---

12 *Meet the Press*, December 9, 1973.
13 There have been innumerable projections; one of the most recent is by Walter J. Levy, Inc., in the London *Economist*, July 31, 1976, p. 61.

aside to gain some incremental business by offering slightly better terms, because that may lead to lower prices all around. Yet they may have no choice in the matter, and most hope that somehow the others will make a little more room for them.

In mid-1976, Venezuela, Libya, Iran, Iraq, and Nigeria were carrying about five MBD of excess capacity. With higher prices, they may carry an even greater burden. If prices were lower, they could not. Lower prices would thus help bring about an outbreak of competition that would result in very much lower prices.

In non-OPEC countries, there is a similar process at work. It is clearest in Norway, a small country with a high standard of living which limits total oil revenues to an amount that the Norwegian economy can absorb without very much disruption. The higher the price, the less the maximum permissible output. If the price fell to half, the Norwegians would permit twice as high a rate of output. Possibly, similar calculations are being made in very different countries, like Mexico and China.

In the United States, Canada, and Australia, high prices reinforce themselves through a political process. High prices would mean windfall gains for the private oil-producing industry. These gains are intolerable to much or most of the citizenry. Accordingly, there are price ceilings on oil. Natural gas price ceilings have existed for years in the United States, but they have never been as important as following the increase in oil prices. All this leads to a curious result in those oil-producing countries which have private oil industries and democratic governments. In Canada and Australia, very high world prices have, if anything, actually diminished investment in production. In the United States, price controls have restrained the expansion.

Thus, for different reasons in different countries, high oil prices have tended to reinforce themselves. Lower oil prices would gather momentum the other way.

The Role of the Oil Companies

The oil cartel nations do not face the difficult, divisive, and probably impossible task of setting production shares. They need not meet together to quarrel over the gain of one being the loss of another. The governments need only agree that they will sell the bulk of their output through the oil companies, whose margins are too narrow to allow any but trifling price cuts.

A cartel is endangered only when more oil is offered than is demanded at the market price. When and if suppliers crowd each other out by offering better terms, and a game of musical chairs begins, the price begins to drop. But the companies cannot put additional amounts on the market at attractive prices to displace a rival who might retaliate by cutting price again. Only the governments can oversupply because only they have the cheap crude. So long as nearly every government refrains from independent offers, the total offered in the market by the companies adds up to the total demanded by consumers at the going price. Then the cartel holds together and can even tolerate a maverick or two. An object lesson came in the Summer of 1974. Saudi Arabia had earned millions of brownie points by announcing a crude oil auction to bring down prices. After getting the maximum publicity, they cancelled the auction.

The market-sharing mechanism of the oil companies is haphazard. It only works with some uncomfortable fluctuations. Occasionally it works badly, and the companies have from time to time actually looked from country to country in search of a better deal on relatively small amounts. But on the whole, the mechanism has worked very well, as shown by the heavy load of excess capacity which it has successfully carried.

Governments and companies today have two problems which upon examination turn out to be really one: company margins for their producing and marketing services, and the differentials between one type of crude and another, reflecting differences in location and quality. For the companies, taking the oil to refine and market, a difference in what they pay for one crude as compared with another must be matched by a difference in what they receive for these crudes. Otherwise, their margin on one crude is greater than on the other, and they cannot tolerate much of a difference. For although these differentials are extremely small in relation to the price of crude oil, they are very large in relation to the company margins, which are only around 25 cents.

These price problems will be serious only if control over supply is weakened. The oil industry generally expects that the surplus will gradually disappear, and that by the mid-1980s at the latest we will have a genuine scarcity on our hands. At least, all countries except Saudi Arabia will be producing flat-out, pushing their reserves as hard as they can, while Saudi Arabia is able to regulate total output and therefore prices by its own decision. Perhaps this is only the latest version of what the oil companies have been saying for the past 30 years, namely, that "rising demand will dry out the surplus." Yet if a skeptic asks, Why should they now be right for the first time? another skeptic could as well ask, Why they should not be right? The fact is that we know too little about the process of discovery and development of oil deposits to have much confidence either way.

The Effects of Vertical Divestiture
on the International Market Structure

Vertical divestiture in the United States would have no effect on the current market structure of international oil. It would have no effect on the control of the OPEC nations over the market. Nothing in the picture would change even slightly if the companies back in the United States were small and nonintegrated. The position of the resident companies would be exactly the same, with no incentive or opportunity to offer more supply at cut prices. Nor would it matter whether the companies aimed to resell the crude or to use it in their non-American refining operations. They could not cut prices either way. "Hard bargaining" by independent refiners, dealing with independent producing companies will not get blood out of the stone—that is, the prices charged by the cartel governments.

Let us try a stronger assumption. If the companies now operating in the producing areas all departed, and were succeeded by independent producing companies, whether American, European, Japanese, or whatever, there would be confusion and lost motion, but nothing more. The Saudis would miss Aramco as an efficient servant, but their market control would be unaffected. So long as the OPEC nations maintain their agreement to sell through the companies at fixed high prices, the cartel will endure. Only the reluctance to face up to the economic problem of the cartel permits these idle daydreams of solving it by company divestiture.

The case against divestiture is so overwhelming that it ought not to be cheapened and diluted with metaphors about "powerful" companies being needed to stand up to the OPEC nations. "Power grows out of the barrel of a gun." Years ago, the tiniest nations showed that they can overpower the biggest companies. Nor do American companies do anything for the security of America's supply. The producing nations make those decisions; and the richer they get, the less they need listen even to other nations, let alone to companies.

Divestiture would slow down the development of new oil supply. It would force the management of every oil company to push to the back burner its projects for exploration and development, in or out of the OPEC nations, as well as its plans for increased recovery from known oil deposits, or the development of nonoil energy sources. The reasons for this distraction and wasted effort are painfully simple. The current value of oil industry fixed assets, revalued into current dollars, is over ten times as great as the investment to be made in any given year. A company ordered to divest most of its assets will serve its stockholders by spending management time on getting the most out of the split-up of existing assets, not on planning for new spending which is only one tenth as large. From the viewpoint of society, this is all wasted effort. Investment in old and new energy sources, on the other hand, is valuable in itself, and may contribute—given political willingness to look at cartel economics—to weakening the cartel.

In the bad old days of Joe McCarthy, many good citizens, alarmed and angry at the Communist threat, whose leaders were far away and invulnerable, relieved their feelings by bashing heads at home. It was not harmless merriment; and the nation paid a heavy price for it. One can only hope that the current rage against the oil companies will pass, as our people look calmly at the mischief done us by the cartel, and seek for defenses against it.

2

Legal and Financial Consequences
of Divestiture

Editor's Note:

The testimony of Peter A. Bator before the Subcommittee on Antitrust and Monopoly of the Committee on the Judiciary of the Senate, which follows, was given on January 27, 1976. His testimony related primarily to S. 2387, the socalled Bayh bill, in the form in which it was then being considered by the Subcommittee. Subsequent to his testimony (and in part in response to certain criticisms and questions raised by him in the course of his testimony) the bill, as reported by the Subcommittee to the full Committee on the Judiciary and by that Committee to the Senate, was amended in several respects. While some of these amendments are of significance, in the Editor's opinion the real substance of Mr. Bator's testimony remains valid in relationship to the bill in the form to be considered by the full Senate. The principal amendments made subsequent to the date of Mr. Bator's testimony and which relate to areas covered by him are as follows:

(a) The original bill would have required the separation of marketing and refining functions. The amended bill permits "major refiners" and "major marketers" to continue these functions, but places a moratorium on further direct operation of retail service stations by any refiner (whatever its size).

(b) The original bill included as "major producers," companies which produced more than 200 billion cubic feet of natural gas in 1974 or any subsequent year. The amended bill

11

is limited to producers of oil, condensate, and natural gas liquids. Thus the amended bill would apply initially to 18 companies, rather than to 20.

(c) The definition of "major refiner" was amended to increase the threshold from 75 million barrels a year to 110 million.

(d) The time period to file divestiture plans with the FTC was increased from 12 months to 18 months and the time period to accomplish divestiture was increased from three years to five years.

(e) The original bill included criminal penalties. The amended bill provides for civil penalties only.

(f) The amended bill includes provisions (not included in the original) for a Petroleum Industry Divestiture Court to "centralize" all litigation relating to divestiture.

(g) Certain of the definitions were changed. Most significant from the point of view of Mr. Bator's testimony, the definition of "control" was altered to cover power or influence over another person arising through "contractual relations which substantially impair the independent business behaviour of another person" rather than power or influence over another person arising through "substantial or long-term contractual relations" and "loans." The effect of this change is to make ambiguous the permissibility of continuing or entering into various long-term contractual undertakings between divested segments of the industry (e.g., a classic throughput agreement between a producer and a pipeline company) rather than explicitly outlawing such arrangements.

Statement of Peter A. Bator, Davis Polk & Wardwell, before the Subcommittee on Antitrust and Monopoly, Committee on the Judiciary, United States Senate—January 27, 1976

Mr. Chairman, I want to thank the Subcommittee for the opportunity granted me to testify today regarding the legal consequences of Senator Bayh's bill, S. 2387, mandating divestiture by certain vertically integrated oil companies. My name is Peter A. Bator and I am a partner in the New York City law firm of Davis Polk & Wardwell. My firm consists of approximately 180 lawyers and carries on a diversified general practice, although our work is to some degree concentrated in the corporate financial area, together with litigation,

Certain Statistics for Companies Apparently Affected by Provisions of US Senate Bill S.2387

Company	Areas Affected by Proposed Legislation[1]				Total Assets[3] ($ million)	Total Long-Term Debt[3] ($ million)	Number of Common Share-holders[3]	Total Stock-holders' Equity[3] (Book Value) ($ million)	Market Value of Common Stock as of 1/16/76[4] ($ million)	Number of Employees
	Annual Domestic Production[2] 36.5MM Barrels or 200 BCF	Annual Refining[2] 75MM Barrels	Annual World-wide Market-ing[2] 110MM Barrels	Trans-portation[2]						
Amerada Hess Corporation	No	No	Yes	Yes	$ 2,255	$ 641	19,196	$ 945	$ 461	5,779
Ashland Oil, Inc.	No	Yes	Yes	Yes	1,716	331	59,368	662	545	27,000
Atlantic Richfield Company	Yes	Yes	Yes	Yes	6,152	1,219	132,863	3,455	4,188	28,800
Cities Service Company	Yes	Yes	Yes	Yes	2,898	569	122,944	1,674	1,123	17,400
Continental Oil Company	Yes	Yes	Yes	Yes	4,673	893	69,192	2,054	3,498	41,174
Exxon Corporation	Yes	Yes	Yes	Yes	31,322	3,052	707,000	15,724	20,243	133,000
Getty Oil Company	Yes	Yes	No	Yes	3,004	158	16,632	1,835	3,185	11,364
Gulf Oil Corporation	Yes	Yes	Yes	Yes	12,503	1,471	372,415	6,329	4,576	52,700
Marathon Oil Company	Yes	Yes	No	Yes	1,860	208	42,891	997	1,332	9,465
Mobil Oil Corporation	Yes	Yes	Yes	Yes	14,074	1,729	226,100	6,436	5,169	73,100
Pennzoil Company	Yes	No	No	Yes	1,798	797	46,303	515	651	9,487
Phillips Petroleum Company	Yes	Yes	Yes	Yes	4,028	658	131,621	2,274	4,342	30,802
Shell Oil Company	Yes	Yes	Yes	Yes	6,129	977	31,917	3,560	3,454	32,287
Standard Oil Company of California	Yes	Yes	Yes	Yes	11,640	1,015	274,000	6,450	5,074	39,540
Standard Oil Company (Indiana)	Yes	Yes	Yes	Yes	8,915	1,427	163,556	5,125	6,139	47,217
Standard Oil Company (Ohio)	No	Yes	Yes	Yes	2,621	805	39,536	1,244	1,925	20,300
Sun Oil Company	Yes	Yes	No	Yes	4,063	679	48,211	2,247	1,152	27,707
Tenneco Inc.	Yes	No	No	No	6,402	2,054	238,275	2,142	2,201	81,000
Texaco Inc.	Yes	Yes	Yes	Yes	17,176	1,897	340,520	9,003	6,854	76,420
Union Oil Company of California	Yes	Yes	Yes	Yes	3,459	648	76,400	1,923	1,442	15,364
					$146,628	$21,228		$74,594	$77,554	779,906

[1] US Senate Bill S. 2387 states that it shall be unlawful for companies to control businesses which qualify under more than one of the following criteria:
(a) *Annual Domestic Production* greater than 36.5 million barrels (100,000 BBL/D) of crude oil, condensate, and natural gas liquids or 200 billion cubic feet (547,945 MCF/D) of natural gas.
(b) *Annual Domestic Refining* greater than 75 million barrels (205,479 BBL/D) of refined products.
(c) *Annual Worldwide Distribution or Marketing* greater than 110 million barrels (301,370 BBL/D) of refined products.
(d) *Domestic or International Transportation* of crude oil or refined products in pipelines.
[2] Based on 1974 data as available from public sources.
[3] As of December 31, 1974, reported in the Annual Report or 10-K of the company.
[4] Calculated as: (Common Shares Outstanding on September 30, 1975, times Closing Common Stock Price on January 16, 1976).

antitrust advice and tax work. My own practice has been largely in the area of corporate financial work, including representation of banks, investment banking firms and corporate clients in connection with securities issues, project financings, acquisitions and so forth.

The firm does not generally represent—that is, we do not act as general counsel or principal outside counsel for—any of the major integrated oil companies as defined in S. 2387. We do act as principal outside counsel for some medium-sized or smaller oil companies, and we do represent from time to time certain of the major integrated oil companies on specific projects, usually on a specific piece of financing or a specific litigation matter. We also advise one of the major integrated companies on a continuing basis on certain tax matters. In addition, through commercial and investment banking clients, my firm and I individually have had substantial experience in advising on the legal aspects of many financing transactions of the major oil companies.

The research on which this statement is based has been done at the request of the American Petroleum Institute, a trade association which has not heretofore been a client of our firm.

I. INTRODUCTION

The purpose of my testimony today is not to discuss the wisdom of divestiture legislation but to try to give the Subcommittee a lawyer's judgment of how a divestiture program would in fact work, and to analyze some of the legal difficulties and problems which would arise if a bill such as S. 2387 were adopted.

I believe such an analysis is useful for two reasons. In the first place, our review of the testimony given before this Subcommittee and other committees indicates that no one has in fact done such an analysis of just how a divestiture program might operate. Second, I believe such an analysis is useful in light of what has been an explicit and important justification given by the proponents of the legislation —that is, that divestiture legislation could solve in a quick, relatively easy and unbureaucratic manner the many problems which are perceived by some to exist in the oil industry.* The inclusion in the

---

*The following statements are taken from either prepared testimony or transcripts of testimony before the Subcommittee during 1975:

"But it is my conclusion that, given the incredible delay inescapably involved in the disposition on a case by case basis of actions filed under the antitrust law, that we would be better off at least selectively by legislation to specify structures that must be dismantled . . .";

bill of a three-year time limit for the completion of divestiture reflects this view. It is easy to say "divest yourself of these or those assets." It is also easy to assume that such a divestiture can be effected speedily and without complications. But the facts are otherwise. My testimony will try to outline the complicated problems that would have to be faced in connection with a divestiture program. My conclusion is that if Congress determines that a divestiture program should be mandated, it will result in a massive amount of litigation and will require ten or more years of great effort by the federal administrative agencies, by the federal judiciary and by the private sector (oil companies, financial institutions and, not the least, lawyers) before divestiture can be accomplished. The process would be a lengthy, arduous and expensive one and would require an extensive revision of existing contractual arrangements underlying the financial and operational structure of the industry. I believe Congress should recognize these factors or run the risk of performing surgery of a most radical nature, and surgery which is irreversible, on the basis of erroneous premises.

In preparation for this appearance, we have reviewed certain documents of a contractual nature from what we believe to be a representative sampling of oil companies affected by the bill, particularly documents relating to the issuance of, and security for, securities issues of these companies. We have also examined the historical pattern of a number of past divestitures, including those occasioned by antitrust litigation and the Public Utility Holding

---

"Without assigning or suggesting an improper motive or indifference to public interest to either of those agencies [the Department of Justice and the Federal Trade Commission], part of the basic problem of any kind of massive judicial procedures seeking antitrust enforcement, the complexity of the cases, the limitation of manpower, consequent limitation in areas that they can in fact move on—all of this has persuaded me that we should seek some legislative, if you will, short cut." (Senator Hart.) "As you know, [the current FTC proceeding] has not even reached the hearing stage, and it is likely to drag on into the 1980s. The time and expense to the Nation can be avoided by Congressional action which can insure that competition is restored now." (Senator Packwood.) "Well, because of the history of this whole antitrust effort—the lack of it—does it not really mandate that the Congress set out specific statutory requirements for how these industries ought to be structured to avoid anticompetitiveness? In other words, just a statute—such as the one we propose today— saying that if you are in this kind of business, you cannot get into that kind of business or if you are this big, you cannot acquire other companies, to avoid all the years of judicial determination and interpretations and consent decrees and so on that slow down and hamper effective antitrust enforcement?" (Senator Abourezk.) "I think it is fairly clear that if we are to have a petroleum industry structured in a form to respond freely and competitively to our needs within a reasonable time, it is up to Congress to take action . . . time is the critical factor." (Mr. Kenneth Cory, Controller, State of California.) "[Divestiture legislation] by its directness and simplicity affirms Congress' clear right to legislate policy without having to delegate implementation of that policy to agencies either reluctant or unable to do the job." (Mr. Patrick, Secretary-Treasurer of the United Mine Workers Union.)

Company Act of 1935. We have made an analysis of the proposed
oil industry divestiture statute under the general theories that have
governed antitrust enforcement in this country. And, of course, we
have analyzed the bill introduced by Senator Bayh on September 23
of last year, S. 2387, as well as reviewing the bill introduced by
Senator Tunney on December 9, S. 2761, and somewhat comparable
amendments offered by Senators Abourezk and Kennedy to the
Natural Gas Emergency Act of 1975, which were defeated in October. We also reviewed the testimony before your Subcommittee
over the past year on the question of vertical integration.

II. ANALYSIS OF S. 2387

A starting point for analysis should be a review of S. 2387. From
the preamble, it is clear that this bill purports to be "antitrust"
legislation, designed to foster competition in the petroleum industry,
since it contains a finding that current antitrust laws have been
inadequate to maintain this competition. The bill then goes on to
define four affected categories of oil companies. "Major producers"
are defined as those which, alone or together with affiliates, produced within the United States in the calendar year 1974, or in any
succeeding calendar year, more than 36,500,000 barrels of crude
petroleum or 200 billion cubic feet of natural gas. In like vein,
"major refiners" are those which, alone or with their affiliates in
any such calendar year, refined within the United States 75,000,000
or more barrels of product, and "major marketers" are those who
alone or with their affiliates in any such calendar year distributed
110,000,000 or more barrels of refined product. Lastly, the bill
defines "petroleum transporters" as those persons using a pipeline
to transport any crude or refined product, without regard to volume.
It is interesting to note that the test for "major marketers" appears
to be worldwide whereas the tests for "major producers" and "major
refiners" are domestic only.

The operative section of the bill makes it illegal after a date three
years from the date of enactment for any company falling within any
of the four categories to own or to control directly, indirectly or
through affiliates any assets used in any of the other processes—
production, refining, transportation or marketing—without regard to
the size of the assets affected or their location (domestic or foreign).
For example, if company X is a "major producer" as defined, it must

dispose of *all* refinery assets, *all* marketing assets and *all* transportation (basically pipeline) assets. The one exception is that "major marketers" are not forbidden from holding interests in refining assets, so long as the size of those refining assets does not make the "major marketer" into a "major refiner" as well. In addition, the bill provides that after the three-year period, no person owning any interest in a producing, marketing or refining asset, of whatever size, will be permitted to transport either crude petroleum or refined products in which it owns an interest through any pipeline which it owns. "Control" is broadly defined to include substantial and long-term contractual arrangements, as well as stock ownership or director interlocks.

In effect, the bill will force divestiture by any company falling within any of the three "major" categories (with the one exception noted) from connection of any kind with the other segments of the oil business both at home and abroad, and will require the complete separation of pipeline assets of whatever size from ownership or substantial contractual connection with the rest of the oil industry.

The bill concludes by giving enforcement authority to the Federal Trade Commission, to which the companies are required to supply, within one year of enactment, plans of divestiture for approval. The Commission's reviewing authority—which includes the power to modify plans submitted by the companies—is based on a "fair and equitable" standard, but no plan is permitted to be approved which would not substantially accomplish the divestiture required by the statute within the three-year period. Willful violations of any provision of the statute are made punishable by substantial fines and imprisonment or suspension of the right to transact business in interstate commerce.

Despite the discussion of the bill in Congress and in the press, it appears that there has not yet been published an analysis of where the strictures of S. 2387 would fall. The Subcommittee recognizes, of course, that all pipeline assets, domestic and foreign, are potentially affected, which means this bill covers more than $9 billion in domestic assets alone owned by approximately 200 oil companies. The companies covered by the provisions of the bill relating to major producers, refiners and marketers are included in the attached chart prepared by Morgan Stanley & Co. Incorporated from public sources. Twenty oil companies appear to fall within the definition of a "major," based on their reported production, refining or marketing volume for 1974. As you can see from the chart, a good many of them are majors in more than one area, and there are no "major marketers" which are not also "major refiners," which means that the exception provided by S. 2387 is meaningless, at least as far as it affects the industry in its current form.

The chart will indicate to you the magnitude of the economic interests which are the subject of the divestiture bills. The total assets of the companies involved amount to more than $146 billion. The aggregate long-term debt of these companies is more than $21 billion. There are hundreds of thousands of people who own the shares and debt securities of these companies directly, and several million more if one counts indirect ownership through pension funds, mutual funds and similar institutions. The aggregate market value of the common stock equity of these companies amounts to more than $77 billion and the companies have some 780,000 employees. If S. 2387 becomes law, it will trigger the largest series of divestitures in history. The assets held by the public utility holding company industry, the only sector of the United States economy even slightly comparable in size that was ever faced with legislative surgery of the kind contemplated here, amounted to a total of only $17 billion in 1935.*

In light of the size of the transactions, the scope of the interests affected, and the potential effects upon United States energy policy and our relations with petroleum producing countries, Congress is under an obligation to examine most carefully and prudently the validity of the major premises which underlie the legislation, and to move cautiously if some or all of such premises are subject to serious challenge. The premise which I propose to challenge is the one that holds that a legislative divestiture program of the type contemplated can be accomplished quickly, easily, inexpensively and unbureaucratically.

III. METHODS OF DIVESTITURE

Assuming legislation such as S. 2387 has been adopted, how would one proceed? How in fact would a major oil company divest itself of various groups of assets and what problems would be raised by any such program?

As a practical matter, there appear to be only two methods for accomplishing the proposed divestiture program. A company can

---

*See 1941 SEC Annual Report at 69-70.

dispose of assets by selling them, whether to another company or to a newly formed company organized and financed for the purpose of acquiring such assets, or to an existing group, such as its own shareholders. In light of the size of the assets to be disposed of, it seem to me—although I am not in any sense a financial expert—extraordinarily unlikely that new capital could be found to finance their purchase. I come to this conclusion at least in part because the requirements of the proposed bill, or the purported aims of divestiture, would not be accomplished if a selling oil company ended up owning the equity securities, or perhaps even the debt securities, of the buyer. In other words, a disposition by way of sale would clearly involve in large part cash, and I cannot believe that a simultaneous disposition of assets of this magnitude by 20 integrated oil companies and of all pipeline assets of approximately 200 companies, could be financed on a largely cash basis, particularly since the most obvious group of buyers, that is the oil companies themselves, would in large part be inhibited by the bill itself or by general antitrust considerations from acting as buyers.

The second and far more likely method of divestiture, and the method often followed in divestitures of major assets required under antitrust decrees, is disposition of such assets in one form or another to the shareholders of the divesting company. This is what is normally referred to as a "spin-off." In its simplest form this means that a company would transfer the assets to be disposed of—we might refer to them as prohibited assets—together with related liabilities to a subsidiary corporation, the shares of which are then distributed as a dividend on a pro rata basis to the shareholders of the company in question. Sometimes the shares, instead of being distributed as a dividend in this manner, are offered to existing shareholders in exchange for shares of the company making the distribution. Sometimes the distribution of shares of the new company owning the prohibited assets is accompanied by a simultaneous reduction in the outstanding equity capital of the distributing company. Whatever specific form a divestiture might take, it seems almost certain that an overwhelming part of the divestiture required by S. 2387 would as a practical matter have to be accomplished through some sort of spin-off of the type I have just described, because payment in cash for the divested assets is not required. Obviously divestiture could be accompanied by sales of some assets by some companies, and in fact it would seem likely that the massive restructuring required by the divestiture bills before you would be accomplished by some combination of disposals by way of sales and various types of spin-offs to existing shareholders.

Having outlined the form of divestiture program might take, let me now try to analyze briefly the contractual and other problems which would be raised by a spin-off plus sale program in the case of any of the oil companies we have under discussion.

IV. LEGAL CONSEQUENCES OF DIVESTITURE

A. *Contractual Arrangements.* In an effort to determine the impact of S. 2387 upon existing contractual relationships, we have reviewed numerous documents relating to a number of oil companies which would be affected by the bill, consisting primarily of (i) indentures pursuant to which the companies have issued notes and debentures to the public, (ii) loan agreements and note purchase agreements with banks, insurance companies, and other institutional lenders, (iii) various documents, such as throughput agreements, charters and leases, which serve as security for, and are the source of payment of, outstanding indebtedness, (iv) concession agreements with foreign governments, and (v) joint venture agreements with foreign governments and others. The major effects of the bill upon these documents may be summarized as follows:

1. *Violation of Covenants.* The documents under which the oil companies have indebtedness outstanding (the "financing documents") contain provisions which prohibit certain actions by the oil companies and which were determined by the respective lenders to be necessary to safeguard their interests. There are a number of types of provisions commonly found in the financing documents which, depending upon the manner in which divestiture is accomplished, may be expected to be violated:

(A) provisions prohibiting an oil company and/or its subsidiaries from selling, conveying or otherwise disposing of (i) particular assets or (ii) a substantial part of its assets;
(B) provisions prohibiting an oil company from selling, conveying or otherwise disposing of the stock of certain of its subsidiaries, most notably its pipeline subsidiaries;

(C) provisions restricting the amount of dividends which an oil company may pay to its shareholders (in those cases where divestiture is accomplished by spin-off, the distribution to shareholders of assets of the magnitude we are considering could be expected to violate such provisions);

(D) provisions requiring an oil company to maintain a certain net worth or a certain ratio of assets to liabilities, or to meet other financial conditions;

(E) provisions requiring an oil company to comply with, or to keep in full force and effect, certain material contracts; and

(F) provisions requiring an oil company to maintain its corporate existence and keep in full force and effect various rights, franchises and licenses.

Attached hereto as Exhibits A through F, respectively, are examples of the various types of covenants referred to above.

Of course, many financing documents contain a number of these provisions. For example, the Sohio Pipe Line Company Note Purchase Agreement dated November 1, 1975, which is one of a series of interrelated financing documents pursuant to which $1.75 billion of the funds required for the construction of the Trans-Alaska Pipeline System has been or is to be borrowed, provides that (i) The Standard Oil Company ("Sohio") will not, and will not permit any subsidiary to, dispose of any part of its net interest in the crude oil reserves in Prudhoe Bay (except under certain circumstances, none of which would include a disposition pursuant to divestiture); and (ii) Sohio will not, nor will it permit any of its subsidiaries to, sell or otherwise dispose of, or part with control of, or offer to sell, any shares of stock of any class of Sohio Pipe Line Company (which owns Sohio's interest in TAPS) to any person other than Sohio or a wholly-owned subsidiary of Sohio. Accordingly, the divestiture by Sohio of its pipeline subsidiary would be a violation of the Note Purchase Agreement, as would a decision by Sohio to divest itself of producing assets.

Violation of the types of covenants referred to above results, either immediately or after a period of time following notice of such violation, in default under the respective financing documents. Such default in turn permits the acceleration of all indebtedness issued thereunder. In addition, many financing documents contain what are called "cross-default" clauses to the effect that the acceleration of any other indebtedness of the oil company itself constitutes a default under the financing documents. Consequently, divestiture of prohibited assets would result in a very substantial portion of outstanding oil company indebtedness becoming subject to acceleration pursuant to the terms of the financing documents. The insistence upon the contractual right to accelerate under such circumstances reflects the creditors' judgments that the occurrence of such violations exposes them to unacceptable risks of nonpayment.

Should S. 2387 become law, the FTC would presumably not permit massive acceleration of oil company debt by allowing creditors to enforce the contractual provisions which they insisted upon as a condition to extending credit to the oil companies and upon which they rely for protection of their investments.* The FTC would instead require that such creditors become debtholders of some or all of the newly formed entities resulting from the divestiture. It would not, however, appear to be "fair and equitable" for the FTC to require existing creditors to accept this new indebtedness without the benefit of any contractual safeguards. As a result, the FTC will be required to determine what contractual provisions should be binding upon these entities in order to adequately protect the interests of such creditors. I will discuss in more detail later the extent of this type of involvement which S. 2387 imposes upon the FTC, and its consequences.

2. *Prohibition of Certain Contractual Relationships.* The bill makes it unlawful for an oil company which is a major producer, refiner or marketer to own or control any transportation asset. The definition of "control" extends to any "direct or indirect legal or beneficial interest in or legal power or influence over another person, directly or indirectly, arising through . . . substantial or long-term contractual relations . . ." As a result, the bill would prohibit the continued existence of various contracts between oil companies and their pipeline subsidiaries which constitute the security for outstanding indebtedness. For example, a very substantial amount of long-term financing has been done in reliance upon the security afforded by throughput agreements and completion agreements between pipe-

---

*It should be noted that S. 2387 is silent as to the ways in which the FTC might act to approve "fair and equitable" plans of divestiture. We have assumed for the purposes of this testimony that the FTC would exercise the power to rewrite contractual provisions and prohibit massive accelerations. Of course, if a court found that the FTC did not have this power, or if the FTC chose not to exercise it, it is clear that divestiture would be followed by default, acceleration and probably the bankruptcy of certain of the companies.

line companies and their parents. Such throughput agreements provide that the parents of the pipeline subsidiaries (i) agree to ship sufficient amounts of petroleum products through the subsidiary's pipeline to enable the subsidiary to satisfy all of its indebtedness, and (ii) in the event sufficient petroleum products are not shipped, agree nevertheless to make available to the subsidiary—as advance payments for future shipments—amounts sufficient to allow the subsidiary to satisfy all of its indebtedness. Under completion agreements the shareholders of a pipeline company agree to advance sufficient funds to the subsidiary (as contributions to capital, subscriptions for additional stock or subordinated advances) to allow the subsidiary to satisfy all of its indebtedness. In each case, the obligation of the parents under these agreements is the source of payment of, and is assigned to the lenders as security for, loans advanced to the pipeline subsidiary. Yet the continued existence of these contracts three years after passage of the bill could well subject the parties to criminal sanctions. Furthermore, a decision by the FTC to permit these agreements to remain in effect after the parent companies divest themselves of their pipeline subsidiaries would, in effect, require the parent companies to make their credit available to an unrelated company in unlimited amounts.* Moreover, in the case of completion agreements it would not be permissible to treat funds advanced by the former parent company as contributions to capital or as subscriptions for additional capital stock (as contemplated by the agreements), and even if one were to consider requiring the former parent company to make such advances as loans, this would still violate the "control" restrictions of the bill since the definition of "control" extends not only to "substantial or long-term contractual relations" but also to "loans."

The bill would also render unlawful the performance of certain existing contracts, including particularly concession and joint venture agreements, which require some combination of producing, refining, marketing or transportation activities. For example, if the terms of a concession agreement require that an oil company both produce and market petroleum products, then the oil company will have to own or control both production and marketing assets in order to perform. The bill, of course, prohibits such ownership or control. The FTC

---

*Throughput and completion agreements customarily define the indebtedness for which the parent is obligated to provide to mean all liabilities of the subsidiary whatsoever, including all indebtedness then existing or incurred thereafter, all taxes, assessments and other governmental charges, all operating expenses and all expenditures for capital items.

might determine that such an agreement should be divided into two contracts to be performed by newly constituted production and marketing entities. It may be, however, that such a division makes no economic sense and the other party may decide that the performance which would be received under such circumstances would not be the performance bargained for. This may be particularly true in the case of concession agreements or joint venture agreements with foreign governments or other foreign parties where it is clear that the foreign entity is looking not only to the actual party to the agreement (which is often a subsidiary formed solely for the purpose of the agreement), but rather to the consolidated group of which the contracting party is a part. Moreover, serious questions are presented as to whether, and under what circumstances, an affected party may be required to enter into separate agreements with newly constituted entities in substitution for a single agreement with one integrated entity which was originally entered into. It does seem quite certain that foreign governments or other foreign entities could not be so required.

3. *Prohibition Against Assignment.* The bill will have a very broad impact on the entire range of oil company contracts to the extent its implementation results in a violation of provisions which generally prohibit the assignment, transfer or conveyance of rights and obligations under such contracts without the approval of the other party. Such violations may be claimed, for example, either because of (i) a sale of the assets necessary for the performance of a contract to a new entity and the assumption by that entity of the obligations under the contract, or (ii) a total change in the stock ownership of the original contracting party. The likelihood of a party asserting such a violation would depend on factors such as (i) the extent to which the party views the integration of the oil company as necessary for the adequate performance of the contract, (ii) whether or not the party sees the contract as advantageous and (iii) the alternatives which the party perceives to exist. While this problem will exist throughout the entire range of contracts, for the reasons set forth above this issue may be most sensitive in the context of concession and joint venture agreements where it may reasonably be expected that it is the resources of the consolidated group which the other party is relying upon. In such cases, newly formed entities may be at a competitive disadvantage with vertically integrated foreign oil companies.

It may also be expected that the implementation of the bill will give rise to claims by some parties that they are excused from the performance of certain contracts on the ground of "commercial frustration"; that is, as a result of an unforeseen and supervening event the performance which the party will receive from newly constituted entities does not have the value bargained for.

B. *Other Problems*. The implementation of the bill will give rise to a number of other serious problems—some or all of which may be susceptible to legislative solution—which do not appear to have received adequate consideration.

Pension Plans. Employees of the oil companies will have a large stake in any divestiture, since it would result in the splitting up of currently integrated oil companies into a number of newly formed entities, each of which would carry on a part of the business formerly conducted with a part of the former employees. This would seem to require a determination as to how to split each existing qualified pension or profit sharing plan into a number of plans. Under the Employee Retirement Income Security Act of 1974 ("ERISA"), vested pension rights of employees are protected by the guarantee of the federal Pension Benefit Guaranty Corporation (the "PBGC"). ERISA also creates a contingent liability in the event that a pension plan is terminated and the value of the plan's benefit guaranteed under ERISA exceeds the value of the plan's assets allocable to such benefits; any such excess is paid by the PBGC, which then has a right to recover such payment from the employer, up to 30 percent of the employer's net worth. Provisions of ERISA designed to state the effect on this contingent liability arising from the sale, merger or division of the employer are ambiguous, and there has as yet been no published interpretation of these provisions by the PBGC or by any other governmental agency or department. If one of the newly formed entities after divestiture should become bankrupt and its pension plan terminated, the PBGC may well contend that the resulting contingent employer liability would be imposed upon all of the newly formed entities and not merely upon the bankrupt entity. Accordingly, even if none of the pension plans of any of these entities is ever terminated, uncertainty may exist as to the nature and extent of the contingent employer liability of each such entity and the form of disclosure to the investing public which would be required under the Federal securities laws.

Tax Consequences. Section 355 of the Internal Revenue Code of

1954, as amended, permits a "spin-off" of assets to stockholders to be done on a tax-free basis provided that certain conditions are met. In such event the stockholders do not recognize a gain or loss on the receipt of the distributed stock of the "spun-off" corporation or corporations, but merely a change in their basis in the stock which they then own. It is not at all clear, however, whether any or all "spin-offs" pursuant to S. 2387 could comply with the provisions of Section 355, and, as a result, such "spin-offs" might have substantially adverse tax consequences for existing oil company stockholders. It is also not clear how much of any mandated divestiture of assets would be accomplished by means of a "spin-off," and the sale of prohibited assets would produce a taxable event for federal income tax purposes. In addition, the transfer of shares of stock or assets may result in the imposition of state and local taxes resulting in further adverse consequences for stockholders and the newly formed entities.

Legal Investment. If the newly formed entities are to obtain necessary funds for working capital and capital expenditures, they will need ready access to the market for the issuance of securities. Various states preclude their savings banks, insurance companies and fiduciaries from investing in securities of certain issuers unless the issuer has a specific ratio of earnings to fixed charges over a specific historical period. It is not clear whether the newly formed entities would be deemed to have been in existence for the necessary historical period within the meaning of such statutes, or how the earnings and fixed charges of the predecessor integrated company would be allocated among the new entities for purposes of such statutes. Failure to satisfy the provisions of these statutes would, as a practical matter, make it difficult or impossible for a large part of the oil industry to obtain financing from institutions governed by such legal investment laws—institutions which have provided a major portion of such financing in past years.

V. FTC INVOLVEMENT:
DURATION AND IMPLEMENTATION

A. *Resolution of Conflicting Interests.* As the foregoing discussion clearly indicates, the divestiture program mandated by S. 2387 would result in a massive, "forced" breach by the oil companies of financing agreements and other contractual arrangements to which they are parties. In other words, forced divestiture of assets along the lines required by S. 2387 could not possibly be accommodated within existing contractual arrangements, and, therefore, such contractual arrangements would have to be "rewritten" by the divestiture plans. In particular, unless the divestiture plans restructured the financing documents of the affected oil companies, divestiture would result in the right of creditors to accelerate and to make immediately due and payable a very substantial portion of the outstanding indebtedness of the affected oil companies.

Thus, the bill will require the FTC to become embroiled in nearly all aspects of the contractual relationships existing between the oil companies and stockholders, creditors, employees and other parties. The FTC will be required to accommodate existing contractual relationships with the newly structured oil industry brought about by divestiture. As a result, the FTC will be required to review, modify and approve plans submitted by the oil companies which, among other things:

    (a) allocate assets and liabilities of existing oil companies among the newly constituted entities;

    (b) restructure the rights of persons holding stock in oil companies and of persons holding options or warrants to purchase such stock or securities convertible into such stock;

    (c) restructure the rights of public and private creditors of the oil companies;

    (d) determine the financial covenants and restrictions which will be imposed upon newly constituted entities to fairly protect the rights of such creditors;

    (e) revise commercial contracts whose provisions no longer make sense under the changed circumstances resulting from divestiture;

    (f) revise existing union and other labor agreements which will probably require renegotiation subsequent to divestiture (presumably "omnibus" union contracts will not be permissible after divestiture); and

    (g) revise employment contracts, pension and profit-sharing plans, leases and insurance policies (or lack thereof since existing oil companies may often choose or be permitted by contract to self-insure, whereas appropriate insurance requirements will have to be determined for new entities).

The complexity of these issues which the FTC will be called upon to resolve must not be underestimated. For example, how does one determine how much of the indebtedness of an existing oil company should be allocated to each of its successor entities? Should the amount of such liabilities be based upon the amount of assets allocated to the entity, the amount of earnings which the entity may be anticipated to generate or some other standard? For purposes of determining the amount of dividends which a new entity will be entitled to declare, how much of the earnings and profits of an existing oil company should be allocated to each successor entity? How should the tax attributes of an existing oil company be allocated; which entities should get the benefits of tax carryforwards and carrybacks, and how does one determine what portion of an existing oil company's previous tax liability a loss carryback may be applied against? What portion of existing pension plan liabilities should each entity assume? Should each successor entity be jointly and severally liable in respect of all outstanding litigation against an existing oil company? How does one allocate contingent liabilities, such as future litigation or tax deficiencies?

Perhaps a specific example of the issues the FTC will face would be in order. Almost all oil company indentures or loan agreements contain provisions to the effect that the company in question will not dispose of all or substantially all of its assets unless the successor company assumes all liabilities and obligations in respect of the indebtedness in question. For some of the affected oil companies, the divestiture required by S. 2387 would involve a group of assets sufficiently large to bring into play such clauses. Holders of the indebtedness in question, or trustees on their behalf, could be expected to argue that such clauses would require each of the successor companies (i.e., the companies owning the assets disposed of) to assume joint and several liability with respect to the indebtedness, so that the holders of the indebtedness could look to each of the successor entities to be responsible for 100 percent of such debt, in case one or more of such entities could not service its allocated portion. It is questionable, however, whether S. 2387 would permit this kind of "cross guarantee" among the entities, in view of the prohibition against control of prohibited assets by way of substantial or long-term contractual relations. On the other hand, the plans as approved by the FTC are required to be "fair and equitable" to all persons concerned, and persons concerned clearly include holders of oil company indebtedness. This is just an example of the kind of problems which the divestiture plans will have to deal with, which the FTC will have to make decisions on and which parties affected are likely to dispute both before the FTC and in the courts.

B. *Accommodation with Federal Governmental Interests.* The bill is silent on another problem facing the FTC: accommodation of other governmental interests. Pipelines, for example, are subject to ICC jurisdiction. Presumably there would have to be some consultation with ICC officials about the proper allocation of pipeline assets in the event of divestiture. A large number of governmental agencies, including the Treasury, the Interior Department and the Department of State, currently have jurisdiction in the general area of energy policy. Would the FTC have to get approval from all of these offices to insure that a particular divestiture did not interfere with general governmental policy in areas such as foreign relations? And, of course, there will be effects upon agencies like the SEC, which will have to resolve how the entities should disclose their confused and tentative status, IRS, which will have to review the plans for tax consequences, and the Defense Department, a large oil buyer and supplier of crude.

C. *Special Problems of Foreign Persons and Governments.* A further and special group of problems will undoubtedly be raised by the requirement of S. 2387 that non-United States assets of the prohibited sort will also have to be disposed of, and "substantial" or "long-term" contractual arrangements relating to foreign prohibited assets will have to be terminated. It cannot be doubted that foreign third parties which have contractual relationships with the oil companies, including foreign holders of oil company indebtedness issued under foreign loan agreements and containing covenants of the kind described above, will seek to enforce their contractual rights in appropriate foreign forums. It can also be expected that foreign courts will support the assertions of such third party foreigners—particularly foreign governments—that their contractual rights cannot be abrogated by unilateral United States action. The result will be, in addition to the loss to the oil companies of valuable foreign contractual rights as a result of termination actions taken by foreign third parties based on "forced" breaches of contract caused by the divestiture program, acceleration of oil company debt held by foreign creditors under loan contracts not governed by US law and claims by foreigners for substantial damages for breach of contract. These claims are likely to be upheld in foreign courts and enforced against the oil companies' foreign assets.

These and a host of other difficult issues must be resolved by plans which the FTC has the responsibility of approving. Moreover, it can be expected that all classes of persons affected by the plans will intervene and participate vigorously in proceedings before the FTC with respect to such plans. Given the number of companies which the bill covers, the difficulty of the issues presented, the large number and variety of classes of persons affected by the bill, the magnitude of the interests involved and the likely event that almost all plans will be submitted to the FTC just before the one year deadline for their submission, one cannot reasonably believe that the FTC will be able to perform the role contemplated for it without the establishment of a new and large bureaucratic apparatus, and even then, the job will take years.

It can also be expected that affected persons will challenge substantially all of the plans submitted to the FTC before the Commission itself and, in addition, will seek judicial review of the FTC's decisions in the Courts of Appeals and the Supreme Court. Indeed, the number and complexity of the issues to be resolved, together with the large numbers of persons whose interests will be affected, virtually insures that the implementation of S. 2387 will give rise to a decade or more of litigation during which substantial uncertainty will exist as to the nature and extent of a broad range of existing contractual arrangements and legal obligations within the oil industry.

VI. PAST DIVESTITURES

When presented with the facts as to the difficulty and farreaching nature of the proposed oil industry divestitures, proponents sometimes point to the Public Utility Holding Company Act of 1935. The administration of the Holding Company Act does provide some instructive history. Although the statute itself provided for time delays to allow for constitutional testing of various provisions, suggesting Congressional awareness of the magnitude of the task and the diversity of interests affected, it was 1946 before the constitutionality of the Act was upheld, and the work of breaking up holding companies continued through the 1960's, although most of it was concluded in the late 1940's and early 1950's. Moreover, a number of factors indicate that the divestiture mandated by the Holding Company Act was far less complex than the divestiture which S. 2387 contemplates:

(i) The magnitude of the undertaking was far smaller—the amount of assets involved and the number and variety of the classes of affected persons was substantially less than would be involved in the oil industry, and the utility industry was entirely a domestic one.

(ii) The assets of the holding companies and subholding companies were not operating assets but largely the securities of operating companies and therefore the break-up of these holding companies did not involve the formidable problem of allocating the assets and liabilities of existing operating companies among a number of newly formed companies.

(iii) The holding companies were in financial disarray in 1935, and thus reorganization was something that would have had to be faced in any event.

(iv) The Holding Company Act did not require the divestment of operating assets by operating companies. The utility industry was essentially a local industry, and viable operating companies with existing management and earnings histories were already in place. Essentially what the Act required was the lopping off of the dead branches of the holding company superstructure, the only purpose of which was to maintain control of the operating companies.

Indeed, the history of the Public Utility Holding Company Act would seem to indicate that even where you have a reasonably carefully drafted statute based on a full record, which was designed to deal with a financially insecure industry far less massive or complex or operationally integrated than the oil industry, the time for divestiture can stretch out beyond 20 years.

But divestiture always takes longer than appears at the beginning. In 1952, for example, the Government settled an antitrust suit against Loew's, Inc. (now MGM) by a consent decree that required divestiture of movie theater assets from movie production assets within two years. Yet, due to difficulties of debt allocation and debtholders' rights, the divestiture was postponed by the court several times, finally being accomplished in 1959, seven years after the date of the decree. And Loew's seemed in 1952 to be a relatively easy company to divide, with assets totalling about $218 million and long-term debt, held by a few insurance companies, of less than $30 million. Other antitrust divestitures, as well as reorganizations resulting from bankruptcies, also indicate the likelihood of extensive time delays.

VII.   COMMENTS ON THE BILL

As I have attempted to demonstrate, the implementation of S. 2387 will give rise to a substantial number of issues of great complexity, the resolution of which will have serious consequences for large classes of persons. In such circumstances, it would not be responsible for Congress to set such events in motion without the most careful consideration and reflection as to the form of legislation which would govern any required divestiture. I respectfully submit that the bill does not evidence the consideration and reflection called for.

For example, a literal reading of the provisions of the bill would require any oil company which is a major producer, refiner and marketer, as defined in the bill, to get out of the oil business altogether. Under the bill, once a company achieves "major" status in an area, it retains such status for all time. Section 4 of the bill provides that a "major" in any one area may not own or control any assets in any other area,* but fails to provide that a company which elects to remain a "major" in only one area must only satisfy the prohibition of Section 4 with respect to a "major" in that area and is in compliance after it has divested itself of all assets in the other areas. For example, assume X Company is a major producer, refiner and marketer and seeks to remain only in the area of production, divesting itself of all other assets. Despite the fact that X Company has divested itself of all refining and marketing assets, it nevertheless remains a "major" refiner and marketer within the wording of the bill. As a consequence, X Company will violate subdivision (3) of Section 4 of the bill, which prohibits major refiners or major marketers from owning any production assets. Indeed, X Company cannot avoid violating the bill if it remains in any area of the oil business.

As discussed above, the bill prohibits a "major" in one area from owning or controlling assets in any other area, and the definition

---

*Subject to the exception, previously noted and not germane to the issue under discussion, that a majority marketer may own "nonmajor" refining assets.

of "control" extends to "substantial" and "long-term" contracts. The bill would, therefore, explicitly outlaw any long-term contractual arrangements between independent producers, marketers, refiners or transporters. Further, any contract between such independent producers, marketers, refiners or transporters that involves more than a small amount of crude oil or other petroleum products would arguably run afoul of the bill's prohibition against "substantial contracts," thereby subjecting the contracting parties to the possibility of criminal sanctions. Despite the fact that S. 2387 is a criminal statute, it provides no definition of "long-term" or "substantial" to guide the companies subject to the bill or the FTC in enforcing the bill. The definition of control contained in the bill seems to go a long way toward prohibiting the kind of contractual relations which would be necessary to allow independent companies to function effectively.

Finally, the bill makes it unlawful for a company to own or control prohibited assets three years after its enactment, and provides no mechanism for an extension of this three-year period. Given the virtual certainty of constitutional challenge to the bill and other substantial litigation surrounding the submission of any plan of divestiture to the FTC for its approval, it seems quite likely that a company attempting in good faith to meet the requirements of the bill may nevertheless be unable to divest itself of all prohibited assets within the prescribed period. If divestiture cannot, as a practical matter, be accomplished within three years, as I believe to be the case, then a statute requiring divestiture to be accomplished within that period, and imposing criminal sanctions for its violation, would be vulnerable to an attack on procedural due process grounds. Nor does the bill make any provision for a company obtaining "major" status during the three-year period following enactment of the bill. For example, a "nonmajor" producer which owns marketing and refining assets might, by virtue of a substantial discovery, become a "major producer" several years after enactment of the bill and face the threat of immediate criminal prosecution unless it can instantaneously divest itself of its prohibited assets.

VIII.   CONCLUSION

Where, then, does this study of legal consequences lead us? The drafting inadequacies of the bill itself raise questions as to whether this kind of simple-sounding legislation is a legally viable approach to disintegrating the largest, and one of the most complex, industries in the world. Moreover, the inevitability of legal challenges to the bill and to its implementation, together with the difficulty and scope of planning and implementing the break-up of all of the major oil companies in the United States, should also make it abundantly clear that any divestiture statute is not at all a simple, swift, unbureaucratic or inexpensive way of resolving what is perceived to be wrong with the oil industry today. In terms of delay, I am not quibbling about the three years in S. 2387 or the five years provided by Senator Abourezk's amendment last October; in my view, it would take at least ten or as long as 20 years to resolve all of the questions raised, from the time of initial submission of divestiture plans to the FTC by the companies, through the review and challenge of those plans and the court tests, to the final carrying out of a divestiture order. The history of the Public Utility Holding Company Act supports this view.

Recognition of these considerations should put to rest the suggestion that a bill like S. 2387 is an appropriate short-cut to the perils of antitrust litigation; no matter what route is selected, the determination of such important questions will of necessity take many years to accomplish. In light of that fact, I believe Congress should recognize what it is giving up in selecting statutorily required divestiture rather than leaving the question to traditional court review and supervision.

A divestiture statute in many ways represents a sharp departure from historical American antitrust approaches. Congress has never before found that size alone, or the vertical integration structure generally, is anticompetitive. Moreover, it has traditionally approached antitrust legislation on an across-the-board rather than single-industry basis. Finally, antitrust law enforcement has been surrounded with procedural safeguards. In divestiture cases, for example, the government has the burden of showing not only that substantial anticompetitive effects have resulted from the alleged conduct and will continue to result in the industry, but also that wide scale vertical disintegration is the best—or, as a minimum, the least harsh—method for overcoming these anticompetitive effects, before the divestiture remedy will be authorized by the court. During the course of litigation bearing on these questions, the court has the benefit of adversary testimony and cross-examination on the premises of anticompetitive effects, as well as expert discussion on the appropriateness of any particular remedy. Although opposing views of witnesses have been presented to the Subcommittee and colloquies have taken place, these issues of effect and appropriateness, as they relate to S. 2387, have never been subjected to the cauldron of a true adversary proceeding.

For example, critics have asserted, and one of the proposed legislative findings in S. 2387 accepts as a premise, that the antitrust laws have been ineffective in curbing anticompetitive abuses in the petroleum industry. Yet there is pending at this very moment an FTC proceeding seeking, among other forms of relief, the vertical disintegration of the eight largest domestic oil companies. At least one source of this proceeding, and one relied on in the bringing of the action, was a 1973 report of the FTC staff which pointed to a number of particular factors which, in the staff's judgment, had reduced competition in the oil industry, among them the oil depletion allowance, oil import quotas, federal tax credits for oil royalties paid to foreign governments and state proration procedures. But since 1973 Congress has eliminated the depletion allowance and severely curbed the use of the foreign tax credit by American petroleum companies, the President has removed the import quotas and state proration limits have become something of a dead letter. The FTC will have to determine, in light of these developments, whether there are serious anticompetitive effects in the petroleum industry, whether any such effects result in large measure from vertical integration or from other causes, and whether the divestiture asked for at the time of initiation of the suit (which, by the way, was far less extensive than the remedy set forth in S. 2387) would still be an appropriate remedy to curb the alleged abuses. Surely, Congress must ask itself whether this FTC proceeding with its built-in adversary safeguards is not a better way to resolve such questions than radical legislative surgery.

Congress should also ask whether it is best to resolve such questions by across-the-board legislation based upon its judgment, at a single time, regarding the industry structure most productive of competition. Antitrust principles have traditionally developed on a case-by-case, rule of reason basis which permits economic, political and social hypotheses to be tested not only in adversary proceedings, but, afterward, by actual experience under a court's decree. Conduct once viewed as anticompetitive may be found in later cases to be appropriate, because of changing views of the law or differing factual circumstances. Moreover, if a remedy proves ineffective or impractical, it may be discarded in subsequent cases; even in cases already decided, if the decreed remedy proves harsh a court may modify the decree. No such possibility of rectifying mistakes or adapting to changing circumstances exists to any meaningful extent when legislation replaces litigation—once divestitures pursuant to statute occur, reintegration could not take place, at least on any short-term basis.

Thus, the selection of the legislative route by Congress brings forth a deep responsibility; it is incumbent upon the legislative branch to use the greatest possible care in passing a statute that can have such extreme consequences as the break-up of all large United States oil companies. It behooves Congress itself to make a full examination of the premises behind the legislative findings backing such a bill, not in haste or in heat, but in reasoned examination of the conduct alleged, the reasonable anticipation of future conduct and the appropriateness, effectiveness and expense of any remedy. Only after such a searching determination should Congress make a legislative finding leading to so drastic a measure, because after passage the Congressional determination will be effectively final.

In addition, Congress must ask itself the question: What happens to this country's energy industry during the ten to 20 years of uncertainty and litigation which will inevitably result from passage of S. 2387? As divestiture programs are proposed by the various oil companies, reviewed and argued before the FTC, litigated by the various interests affected, this enormously complex and vital sector of our industrial economy will be in what amounts to a state of chaos. Until plans are finally approved, litigation concluded and plans put into effect, literally no one will know who owns what, what kind of companies will merge, what their capital structure will look like or how viable and competitive, both domestically and overseas, the fragmented components will be. Congress must carefully consider whether an industry in this state of uncertainty could finance on a private basis the huge capital-intensive projects which any national energy policy for this country requires.

Exhibit A
Restrictions On Disposition Of Assets

So long as the Production Payment remains in force and effect [Oil Company] will not, without the consent in writing of [Lender], sell, convey, assign, lease, sublease or otherwise dispose of any

Subject Interest (or any portion thereof) or release, surrender or otherwise abandon any Subject Interest (or any portion thereof) . . .

If any of the following events ("Events of Default") shall occur, namely, if:

the Charterer and/or [Oil Company] ceases or threatens to cease to carry on its business or (without the prior written consent of [Lender] . . .) disposes or threatens to dispose of a substantial part of its businesses, properties or assets or the same are seized or appropriated;

[Oil Company] covenants and agrees that from the date of this Guaranty Agreement and thereafter so long as [Lender] holds any of the Notes, [Oil Company] will not . . . sell, lease, transfer or otherwise dispose of all or a substantial part of its properties and assets, or consolidate with or merge into any other corporation or permit any other corporation to merge into it . . .

Exhibit B
Restrictions On Disposition
Of Stock Of Subsidiaries

[Oil Company] will not, nor will it permit any of its subsidiaries to, sell or otherwise dispose of, or part with control of, or offer to sell, any shares of stock of any class of [subsidiary] to any Person other than [Oil Company] or a wholly-owned subsidiary of [Oil Company], or entertain any offer from any Person other than [Oil Company] or a wholly-owned subsidiary of [Oil Company] to purchase any shares of stock of any class of [subsidiary], and [Oil Company] will not permit [subsidiary] (either directly, or indirectly by the issuance of rights or options for, or securities convertible into, such shares) to issue, sell or dispose of any shares of any class of its stock except to [Oil Company] or to a wholly-owned subsidiary of [Oil Company].

[Oil Company] covenants and agrees that from the date of this Guaranty Agreement and thereafter so long as [Lender] holds any of the Notes, [Oil Company] will not . . . fail at any time to own all of the outstanding capital stock (other than directors' qualifying shares) of [subsidiary] either directly or through one or more of its wholly-owned subsidiaries . . .

[Oil Company] will not sell, transfer or otherwise dispose of any voting shares of [pipeline subsidiary] of any class to any person and will not permit [pipeline subsidiary] to issue, sell or otherwise dispose of any of its voting shares of any class to any person other than [Oil Company] . . .

Exhibit C
Limitation On Dividends

[Oil Company] will not pay any dividend (other than stock dividends) on any of its stock and [Oil Company] will not, and will not permit any of its Subsidiaries to, make any payment on account of the purchase, redemption or other retirement of any of the [Oil Company's] stock or make any other distribution in respect thereof (each such dividend, payment and distribution being herein called a "stock payment"), except that [Oil Company] may make any stock payment if after giving effect thereto the aggregate amount of all stock payments made after December 31, 1974 shall not exceed the sum of (1) the consolidated net profit, after taxes and extraordinary items, of [Oil Company] and its Consolidated Subsidiaries for the period from December 31, 1974 to the date of the making of such stock payment, such period to be taken for the purpose as one accounting period (except that consolidated net profit after taxes and extraordinary items shall be calculated exclusive of a charge estimated as of June 1, 1975 to be [dollar figure], currently proposed by the Financial Accounting Standards Board, to provide deferred income taxes on capitalized intangible drilling costs incurred to January 1, 1975, which costs were previously deducted for Federal income tax purposes) plus (2) $30,000,000.

[Oil Company] will not declare or pay any dividends (except dividends payable in common stock of the Company) or make any other distribution on any shares of its capital stock of any class or make any payment on account of the purchase, redemption or retirement for value (other than with the proceeds of additional stock financing) of any shares of such stock, if the Net Working Capital of [Oil Company] (as at the end of a calendar month not more than 50 days prior to the date of such declaration, payment or distribution) shall, after giving effect to such declaration, payment or distribution, be thereby reduced below the greater of (x) the sum of $2,000,000 or (y) an amount equal to one-half of the principal amount of the Funded Debt of [Oil Company] that becomes due and payable . . . during the 12 months' period commencing at the end of such calendar month.

Exhibit D
Maintenance Of
Financial Requirements

[Oil Company] will, on or before   in
each year beginning with the year   , deliver to the person to
whom the Notes were originally issued, and lodge at the office of
[Oil Company] and make available for examination purposes at said
office to any other holder of the Notes, a Certificate of [Oil Company]
(herein referred to as the "Annual Net Tangible Assets Certificate")
stating, at the close of business December 31 (herein referred to as
the "Determination Date") of the year immediately prior to the year
in which said Certificate is made, the following:

> that the Net Tangible Assets of [Oil Company] on the
> Determination Date are at least equal to 2½ times the amount
> of Funded Debt of [Oil Company] on said date; or, in the
> alternative, stating that the Net Tangible Assets of [Oil Com-
> pany] on the Determination Date are a specified amount less
> than 2½ times the amount of Funded Debt of [Oil Company]
> on said date.

[Oil Company] will not, and will not permit any Consolidated
Subsidiary to, create, assume or permit to exist any senior funded
debt unless after giving effect thereto (and to the application of
proceeds thereof) the consolidated senior funded debt of [Oil Com-
pany] and its Consolidated Subsidiaries shall not exceed 75 percent of
the consolidated Tangible Net Worth of [Oil Company] and its Consolidated Subsidiaries.

[Oil Company] will continuously maintain a Net Worth of not
less than $1,500,000. For purposes of this § . . . : "Net Worth"
means its net worth at and as of the particular date, composed of the
sum of all amounts, determined in accordance with generally accepted
accounting principles, which would properly appear on its balance
sheet dated such date as (A) the par or stated value of all outstanding paid-in capital stock and (B) capital, paid-in and earned surplus
(a negative amount, in the case of a deficit), less the sum of (C)
any surplus or write-up resulting from any reappraisal of any property
or asset, (D) any amounts at which good will, patents, trademarks,
copyrights and deferred charges, including but not limited to unamor-
tized debt discount, debt expenses and organization expenses, but
not prepaid expenses, appear on the asset side of such balance sheet,

(E) any amounts at which shares of its capital stock appear on the asset side of such balance sheet, (F) any amounts of indebtedness not included on the liability side of such balance sheet and (G) the amount of any net worth otherwise required to be set aside or reserved by it pursuant to any law or regulation or any agreement or instrument.

Exhibit E
Compliance With
Certain Agreements

[Oil Company] will perform and observe all agreements, covenants and undertakings of [Oil Company] contained in the Completion Agreement, the Throughput Agreement and the related . . . Assignment, and will not consent to any amendment or termination of the Completion Agreement or the Throughput Agreement except as provided therein

[Oil Company] will promptly . . . perform or cause to be performed each and every act, matter or thing required by, each and all of the leases to which [Oil Company] is a party or in which it has any interest and will do all other things necessary to keep unimpaired [Oil Company's] rights thereunder and prevent any default thereunder or any forfeiture of any rights of [Oil Company] in respect thereof . . .

Exhibit F
Maintenance Of
Corporate Existence

[Oil Company] covenants and agrees that so long as any of the Notes shall be outstanding [Oil Company] will do or cause to be done all things necessary to preserve and keep in full force and effect its corporate existence . . .

[Oil Company] will take or cause to be taken all such action as from time to time may be necessary to maintain, preserve or renew its corporate existence.

3

Charges of Domestic Energy Monopoly: The Dog in the Manger of US Energy Policy

EDWARD W. ERICKSON

Introduction

It is not uncommon for an unwarranted degree of homogeneity to be attributed to a nominal entity which is in fact a collection of disparate parts. An historical example is the "monolithic Sino-Soviet bloc." A more current one is "United States energy policy." Energy is not homogeneous. Political tension exists. Energy has always been a policy area in which political stress lines are particularly evident.[1] US energy policy is only consistent in its failure to come to grips with the central realities of our circumstances.

These central realities are: (1) the world energy economy will be primarily fired by conventional fossil fuels for the foreseeable future, and the United States will not be an exception; (2) oil is the premier fossil fuel in terms of availability and flexibility of use, and the minimum incremental cost of additional oil to the US energy economy

---

1 See, for example, the editors' introductions and contributed essays in E. W. Erickson and L. Waverman, eds., *The Energy Question, An International Failure of Policy* (Toronto: University of Toronto, 1974).

is the OPEC price;[2] and (3) the United States is and will remain primarily a market-organized economy, and the principal agents of US society for energy production and distribution will be the integrated major oil companies.

A new balance has been struck in world energy markets. The world price of oil has risen dramatically. The OPEC marker price for Saudi Arabian light crude oil is the benchmark from which the cost and benefit calculations for any nation's energy policy must begin.[3] There are unavoidable questions regarding the stability of the Saudi price. Will it remain relatively stable in nominal terms, and thus erode in real terms? Will it be indexed so that it increases in nominal terms? If it is indexed, will the indexation cause world oil prices to remain relatively constant or to increase in real terms? Do the Saudis have the resource base and reserve potential to establish sufficient productive capacity to maintain their leadership role in OPEC? Will the OPEC price break in nominal terms, and if so, to what level and for how long? These are imponderables which must influence the formation of energy policy in any country, but they all start with and ultimately come back to the Saudi price.[4] It is against current reality and future expectations concerning the Saudi price that energy policy affecting production, consumption, strategic storage, and international relations must be made.

The United States has not fully incorporated the new reality concerning world oil prices into the set of signals through which energy policy is made and implemented. The principal resource allocation mechanism in the United States is the market system. Even public

---

2 In terms of its effect on the demand for imports, a barrel of oil conserved is the equivalent of a barrel of additional domestic production. There are now opportunities to "create" barrels of oil through conservation efforts. The initial barrels saved may have a cost in terms of the expenditures necessary to conserve them which is less than the price of imported oil. In this sense, conservation can yield relatively inexpensive oil. Ultimately, however, the cost of creating oil by conservation would equalize with the cost of conventional oil supplies. In the United States, the regulation of oil and natural gas prices does not now encourage optimal price-induced conservation. Even if regulation did not subsidize wasteful energy consumption, however, it is likely that price-induced conservation would only slow the rate of growth of energy demand, not cause it to decrease in absolute terms.

3 For a discussion of the world oil market and the special role which the Saudis appear currently to be playing, see E. W. Erickson and H. S. Winokur, Jr., *Nations, Companies and Markets: International Oil and Multinational Corporations* (Fraser Institute, forthcoming).

4 In focusing upon the Saudi price, I do not mean to imply that the possibility and consequences of a future oil embargo should be disregarded. Rather, I am primarily concerned with economic considerations. An embargo would certainly have economic impacts. But any economic benefits which an embargo would generate for OAPEC could be achieved by less costly means. The contingency planning surrounding embargo possibilities is, therefore, primarily a response to political factors.

policy is largely implemented through the market.[5] Market signals are prices. US energy production is less than it could be, US energy consumption is greater than it should be, and US oil imports are growing rapidly because the United States is unwilling to allow domestic energy prices to reflect the new reality of world oil prices. It would be possible to argue on national security grounds that US energy prices should exceed the level consistent with world oil prices; but it is impossible to argue on either economic efficiency or national security grounds that US energy prices should be *below* world oil prices.

Domestic energy prices are now below levels consistent with world oil prices. This is especially true for oil and natural gas. It is possible that, at the end of the 39-month period of gradual US crude oil price escalation mandated by the Energy Policy and Conservation Act of 1975, the difference between world oil prices and both new and average US oil prices will be greater than it was at the end of 1975. The relative price differential between the United States and the world markets does not represent an abundance of indigenous, low cost, US energy resources. Quite the contrary. Despite the price differential, oil imports into the United States are growing in both absolute volume and as a fraction of domestic consumption.[6] Such a situation might be unavoidable. If so, it must be recognized as a fact of nature in a context which involves appropriate national security and strategic storage contingency planning. Increasing absolute and relative import dependence should not be an unconscious result of a haphazard set of makeshift improvisations masquerading as a US energy policy.

Unfortunately, increased US import dependence is now the case in part as a result of a policy vacuum. A policy can be a sum of component parts. A policy can also consist of *not* taking some action. In these respects, the United States has an energy policy.

The action we are not taking is a rationalization of the incentives to produce and consume energy in the United States with the world price of oil. The world price of oil is the minimum long-run cost of incre-

5 For an analysis of a proposal which relies upon market incentives and private initiatives to attempt to achieve maximum efficiency, flexibility, and planning focus for national security strategic storage, see Daniel H. Newlon and Norman V. Breckner, *The Oil Security System: An Oil Import Policy for the United States,* Research Contribution 255 (Institute of Naval Studies, Center for Naval Analyses, January 1974).

6 In late August 1976, imports of crude and products into the United States were running at an annual rate of 7.2 million barrels per day. This was up over ten percent from a year earlier, and represented over 40 percent of US demand. *Oil and Gas Journal,* August 30, 1976, p. 91.

mental energy supplies to the US ecohomy. Not to acknowledge this fact in the set of current domestic market signals which affect daily consumption and production and longer-term investment decisions for energy-using and energy-producing capital has a number of consequences. First, there is a domestic misallocation of resources. Second, increased import dependence increases strategic and political vulnerability. Third, to pay for oil imports, we export goods and services which, at the margin, are more valuable to us than the incremental consumption associated with the incremental barrels of oil imported. Fourth, we contribute to circumstances which increase the probability that the world price of oil will be higher, or increase at a more rapid rate. And fifth, delaying the adjustment process increases the ultimate cost of adjustment.

If there are any consistency principles which bind together the component parts of our actions, two candidates are (1) a feeling that any step which appears to be a concession to the US oil industry is to be taken with the utmost reluctance, and (2) a mistaken belief that any measure which disrupts the organization or impedes the activities of the major oil companies can be taken with no adverse consequences in terms of investment planning, operating costs, and domestic supply. Examples of this outlook include *FTC vs. Exxon, et al.*, proposals for vertical divestiture of firms in the US petroleum industry, proposals for horizontal disintegration of energy companies, the fact and form of crude oil and refined products price regulation, the continued regulation of the wellhead price of interstate natural gas sales, and restrictions on joint bidding by major firms in offshore OCS (outer continental shelf) lease sales. Such policies are inconsistent with a well-defined conception of the national interest and with the principle that private energy companies are the agents through which society implements a market-oriented national energy policy. They are not inconsistent with an overall national energy policy which is less than the sum of its parts, nor with a deep set of social stress lines which originate in political tension regarding the role, behavior, and performance of the US oil industry in general and the major oil companies in particular.

Competition

The question of competition is central to the problem of why we behave as we do, or how we rationalize our behavior. If one is to depend upon the reaction to market signals for implementation of a major portion of national policy, then better social results are achieved if the markets through which policy goals are achieved are competitive. There are generally two explicit lines of argument as to why the United States behaves so reluctantly in coming to grips with the central realities of the situation with which a consistent, cohesive, and constructive national energy policy must cope. The principal initial commitment of such a policy would be to rationalize the relationship between the world price of oil and US energy prices. Such rationalization would involve US energy prices which were in market equilibrium with US oil prices.[7] Domestic oil prices, in turn, must at least be equal, across the board, to the world price of oil. Because of the threat of embargo, a combination of strategic storage and tariff- or quota-induced differentials between the US and the world price are also justified.

The first explicit reason why the United States has been reluctant to allow US energy prices to equilibrate with US oil prices which are only just equal to the world oil price is because of charges of monopoly in energy markets. The second explicit reason why an appropriate rationalization of US and world energy price regimes has not been permitted to occur has been the issue of windfall profits. A third, implicit, reason why it has been so difficult for the United States to initiate a forward-looking, prospective national policy is the basic antagonism that so many appear to hold toward the oil industry in general, and the major firms in particular. This antagonism seems to originate in a long and deeply-held populist logic which argues that bigness is badness, monopoly is badness, therefore bigness is monopoly. Under current circumstances, the populist logic is also entwined with the issue of windfall profits. But the windfall profit problem can be relatively easily solved with appropriate tax policy. Even if the rationalization of US and world energy price regimes were contained in an omnibus legislative package which also included appropriate tax policy, it is likely that it would be opposed on grounds of monopoly.

The question of monopoly in the US oil and gas industry, and the discussion it engenders, is confusing. One aspect of the confusion involves the distinction between the US and world markets. The

---

7 This is not now the case. The regulation-induced shortage of natural gas in interstate markets is evidence of persistent disequilibrium in domestic US energy markets.

OPEC and other oil-exporting countries are enjoying the exercise of market power in the world oil market. The exercise of this market power is intimately bound up with the role of Saudi Arabia as dominant price leader.[8] The increase in price-determined rents accruing to oil-exporting countries has exceeded the increase in the price of world oil. The volatility in the market shares of countries is not consistent with either an explicit prorationing system operated by OPEC itself or one implicitly enforced by the companies.[9] As nationalization and the development of state oil companies in the OPEC countries proceeds, the multinational oil companies are coming more and more to fill primarily the role of service contractors and conduits for the world flow of oil. The implications of the statement attributed to the Shah of Iran—"With the sisters controlling everything, once they accepted everything went smoothly"[10]—are incorrect now, and were inconsistent with the events which preceded it over the decade of the 1960s. If the majors controlled everything, then it certainly was not in their interest to allow the secular erosion in the real price of oil in world markets which characterized the 1960s. One must not miss the critical point. It is no accident that the OPEC marker price is Saudi Arabian light. There is now a substantial element of monopoly rent in the world price of oil, but it is not because the companies control everything. The Saudis are in the dominant position.

It is, therefore, appropriate to separate the question of nation-state monopoly power in the world market from that of whether or not the domestic US market is competitive. For the purpose of the present discussion, it is taken as given that the OPEC price reflects the exercise of market power, and Saudi Arabia is the linchpin of the system. The monopoly is one of countries, not companies. The questions we may then address are the more relevant ones from the standpoint of national energy policy: (1) Is there any evidence of monopoly power on the part of private companies in the domestic energy markets of the United States? and if so, (2) How should such market imperfections affect our willingness to rationalize the world and US energy price regimes?

Examination of questions concerning competition or monopoly

---

8 See Erickson and Winokur, *op. cit.*
9 *Ibid.*
10 Anthony Sampson, *The Seven Sisters, The Great Oil Companies and the World They Shaped* (New York: Viking, 1975).

focuses upon three related areas: structure, behavior, and performance. Market structure refers to the number and size distribution of firms in an industry. Economic behavior involves the manner in which firms in an industry interact with each other and with the physical and institutional environment. Economic performance involves the degree to which criteria for efficient resource allocation are met. Because the eight largest US petroleum firms are currently the respondents in a suit filed by the Federal Trade Commission, the discussion here will be particularly concerned with these firms.[11] Economic performance, the basic concern, is addressed first. Then the structure of the US petroleum industry is examined. Finally, two critical aspects of the behavior of the industry—joint bidding in offshore lease sales, and banked costs—are discussed.

The rationale for selecting these particular behavioral aspects of the industry is twofold. First, the Department of the Interior has recently issued regulations which prohibit the largest firms from bidding jointly with each other in offshore OCS lease sales. Presumably this was intended to correct some competitive deficiency, and hence it is worthwhile to examine whether there was, in fact, a deficiency to correct.

Second, much of the examination of the structure and performance of the industry relies upon data which covers the relatively tranquil historical period prior to the Arab oil embargo of 1973. This is appropriate because it is desirable to get a feel for the competitive processes at work in the industry prior to the disequilibrium created by the embargo and the controls and regulations imposed upon the industry. Price controls began to distort the efficiency of resource allocation in the US petroleum industry in the early 1970s, and are still in force. The industry is still not fully adjusted to the shocks generated by the embargo.[12] Thus, the data of the 1950s and 1960s

---

11 The respondents in *FTC vs. Exxon, et al.*, are Exxon, Standard Oil Company of Indiana, Texaco, Gulf, ARCO, Standard Oil Company of California, Mobil, and Shell. This is a smaller set of firms than those which would be directly affected by the divestiture legislation now before the US Senate, but all of the respondents in *FTC vs. Exxon* would be subject to divestiture under the proposed provisions of the Senate bill. The actual number of firms that might be directly affected by legislative divestiture action is unclear. Whatever the fate of the Senate bill (S. 2387), the FTC suit can be expected to be pursued. Part of the relief sought by the FTC is divestiture of refining and marketing from other operations. For reasons of precision and clarity, I therefore focus on the respondents in the FTC suit. But the arguments developed here would also apply to the larger set of firms which might be labeled as "all majors."

12 The lag adjustment process for reserves is relatively slow. The long-range exploration and development process through which reserves are added is both time- and capital-intensive. See E. W. Erickson, S. W. Millsaps, and R. M. Spann, "Oil Supply and Tax Incentives," *Brookings Papers on Economic Activity* (Brookings Institution, February 1974), pp. 449-478.

—a period of gradual growth, expansion, and competitive adjustment to changing market conditions in the industry—are particularly relevant. But it is also desirable to examine some evidence on the competitive processes at work which originates in the more recent regulated period. For this reason, industry behavior with respect to a special provision of the domestic product price control scheme— banked costs—is especially interesting.

Performance

In a market-oriented economy, profits are a critical element in the signal and response system through which the resource allocation process operates.[13] When profits are high in a given activity, it is a signal that it is worthwhile on a social basis to allocate more resources to that activity. In a competitive environment with mobile resources and an absences of barriers to resource flows due to either regulation or monopoly, relatively high profits induce resource reallocation until the prospective marginal social benefits from additional resources devoted to the endeavor in question are no longer sufficient to justify the marginal social opportunity costs. Profitability is thus an index of the social urgency of devoting resources to particular activities.

Profitability is also an important index of the existence and exercise of market power. The petroleum industry is a large industry, and the firms within it are also large. Effective monopoly results in a divergence between long-run marginal costs and prices. Prices in excess of long-run marginal costs (including a competitive return on invested capital) result in excessive earnings. These excessive earnings are reflected in higher-than-normal, above-average rates of return on stockholders' equity capital. Thus, the rate of return on corporate stockholders' equity capital is one measure of the presence or absence of market power in the petroleum industry.

There are thus two important questions concerning the profitability of the US petroleum industry. First, do the long-run profitability data suggest that there are any systematic divergences from effective competition, so that market-directed resource allocation might yield imperfect social results? And second, do the short-run profitability data for recent years indicate that increased investment in domestic energy supplies is an activity of high social urgency?

---

13 Parts of this section follow E. W. Erickson and R. M. Spann, "The US Petroleum Industry," in Erickson and Waverman, eds., *op. cit.*, vol. 2, *North America*, pp. 5-24.

Market power shows up as economic profits. The US petroleum industry has not earned the kind of long-run returns on stockholders' equity which are to be expected for firms that enjoy substantial, systematic market power. This index of effective competition yields positive results whether the comparison is to all US manufacturing, Moody's 125 Industrials, Moody's 24 Public Utilities, or a group of industrial firms likely to possess market power, or to the cost of equity capital for the petroleum industry.

Table One compares the overall average profitability of the eight major petroleum companies named in the FTC complaint (see fn. 1) with ten large industrial concerns generally conceded to possess some market power. The years considered are 1971-72, because these are years of approximate equilibrium in world oil markets prior to the OPEC price explosion. The comparison indicates that each of the nonpetroleum firms earns more than the average for the eight major petroleum companies. The average for the ten nonpetroleum firms

Table One
A Comparison of Rates of Return on Stockholders' Equity Between Ten Selected Large Firms in Concentrated Industries and the Eight Major Petroleum Companies

Firm	Rate of Return on Stockholders' Equity, 1972 (Percent)
General Motors	17.8
Xerox	23.4
IBM	18.7
Burroughs	15.4
Bristol-Myers	17.8
Eastman Kodak	20.4
Kellogg	22.3
Procter and Gamble	19.1
Pfizer	17.7
Eli Lilly	29.8
Ten-Company Average	20.2
Average for Eight Major Petroleum Companies (1971)	11.1

Table Two
Comparisons of Rates of Return

Year	Moody's 125 Industrials (Percent)	Eight Largest Petroleum Firms (Percent)
1971	11.2	11.1
1970	10.2	10.8
1969	12.2	10.8
1968	13.0	12.4
1967	12.4	12.4
1966	14.2	11.6
1965	13.7	12.1
1964	13.3	10.5
1963	12.4	11.5
1962	11.6	10.7
1961	10.5	10.4
1960	10.8	10.2
1959	11.6	9.8
1958	10.2	9.6
1957	13.2	13.1
1956	14.3	14.1
1955	15.4	13.7
1954	13.2	12.8
1953	13.4	13.9
1952	13.2	13.6
1951	14.6	15.3

is 20.2 percent. The average for the eight major petroleum companies is 11.1 percent. The ten-company nonpetroleum average exceeds the average for the eight major petroleum companies by 9.1 percentage points, or 82 percent.

Table Two compares the rate of return on stockholders' equity for the eight major petroleum companies with the average for Moody's 125 Industrials on a year-by-year basis from 1951 through 1971. In 16 of 21 years, the average for the eight major petroleum companies is less than that for the firms that make up Moody's 125 Industrials. Moreover, in eight of the ten years covering 1962-71, the rate of return for the eight major petroleum companies was less than the return for Moody's 125 Industrials. In one year, 1967, they were equal. In only one recent year, 1970, did the return for the eight major petroleum companies exceed that of Moody's 125 Industrials—and then by only six-tenths of one percentage point, or 5.8 percent.

In the 11 years prior to 1962, the rate of return for the eight major petroleum companies exceeded the rate of return for Moody's 125 in only three years. These were the consecutive years 1951, 1952, and 1953. On average, then, the long-run trend over this period in the return on stockholders' equity for the eight major petroleum companies has been down relative to Moody's 125 Industrials. To the extent that decreased long-run profitability is an index of increased competition, the profitability indices indicate that the petroleum industry has been becoming more rather than less competitive. (This indication is consistent with, for example, the record of entry into foreign operations and offshore activity.)

Comparison to averages such as Moody's 125 Industrials and all manufacturing industry may be misleading. This is because some of the nonpetroleum firms in these averages may possess market power (see, for example, Table One). This makes the averages themselves higher than the normal, long-run, competitive rate of return. There is a way to correct for this.[14] A standard procedure in regulatory proceedings is to calculate the cost of equity capital for the particular firm(s) in question. Earnings on equity capital are then compared to the cost of equity capital.

Modern analysts typically calculate a range for the cost of equity capital. This is because a range is more reliable than a point estimate. Using standard techniques for the years 1967-71, the range for the cost of equity for the eight major petroleum companies is 10.3 to 12.3 percent.[15] The midpoint of this range is 11.3 percent.

---

14 Another correction would involve accounting procedures. Unless accounting conventions are standardized across industries, ambiguities may result. Unfortunately, the most general thing that may be said about standard accounting conventions is that they are not standard. For example, if proved oil, gas, and coal reserves and domestic real estate are undervalued on energy company balance sheets with respect to similar items on the balance sheets of companies in other industries, the effect may be to overstate the profitability of energy companies. But problems with the balance sheet valuation of assets are not limited to the energy companies. Were one to make a one-time adjustment for energy companies, one would also have to do so for such companies as, for example, IBM. Although there would be some changes in absolute magnitudes, it is not clear that the pattern of comparison would change.

15 The discounted cash flow method was used to calculate both of these estimates. The 10.3 percent calculation is the sum of the average 1971 dividend yield for the eight companies plus the average five-year growth rate in earnings per share. The 12.3 percent estimate was derived by substituting the average beta factor for the eight major petroleum companies (0.95) into a regression equation which related DCF estimates of the cost of equity capital for electric utilities to their beta factors.

For this same 1967-71 period, the average earnings on stock-holders' equity for the eight major petroleum companies were 11.5 percent. Within the limits of the precision of such calculations, the earnings on stockholders' equity (11.5 percent) and the cost of equity capital (11.3 percent) are approximately equal. This is what we would expect in an effectively competitive industry operating in an economy with well-functioning capital markets. The rate-of-return data indicate that the eight major petroleum companies are part of a competitive industry and are themselves earning the competitive rate of return. If simple monopoly power or more complex collusive behavior were an important feature of the petroleum industry, one would expect it to show up in the long-run rate-of-return data. It does not.

The earnings of US oil companies in recent years have been higher than their long-run averages. This is for a number of reasons. The fundamental driving force has been the higher world price of oil engineered by OPEC. The ramifications of this fundamental force have shown up in a variety of ways, including transitory inventory profits, foreign exchange earnings, and other essentially accounting considerations. But there is a basic thrust at work. This basic economic thrust is the brute fact that changed world circumstances have made domestic energy resources more valuable. The recent profit experience of the major US petroleum companies indicates that the private market puts a high social urgency upon the creation of additional domestic energy capital.

Table Three shows net income as a percent of stockholders' equity for the eight largest companies for the first half of 1976. The average rate of return is 14.1 percent. This is 2.2 percentage points, or 18 percent, higher than the long-run average for the 1951-71 period. If crude oil and refined product prices were completely decontrolled and at least partially rationalized with respect to world prices, the oil company earnings figures reported here would be increased. This is evidence that government controls suppress the market signals which would otherwise give us a clear index of the social urgency of incremental domestic energy supply investments. Since higher earnings would be associated with higher prices, government controls which restrain prices also distort the signals individual consumers receive with respect to the social value of self-initiated, price-induced conservation.

Table Three
Short-Run Profitability of Leading Petroleum
Companies for the First Half of 1976

Company	Net Income as a Percent of Stockholders' Equity
ARCO	14.7
Exxon	15.6
Gulf	12.6
Mobil	12.5
Shell	18.8
Standard Oil of California	12.0
Standard Oil of Indiana	16.9
Texaco	9.8
Average	14.1

Source: American Petroleum Institute, as reported in *Oil and Gas Journal,* August 30, 1976, p. 24.

Through price controls we socially intervene in the energy market. This intervention perversely distorts market signals with respect to the social costs and benefits of additional energy consumption and production. One of the reasons we persist in our delusions appears to be a fundamental aversion to oil company profits. A potential remedy to this impediment will be discussed below. But at least two things are evident from an inspection of oil company profit data and the environment within which these data are generated. First, the long-run record is one of an effectively competitive industry. Second, the recent increase in profitability is an index of the social urgency of additional domestic energy supply investments, and this index is an understatement of the true social value of such investments.

Structure

The traditional starting place in a discussion of market structure is the degree to which production, sales, or assets are concentrated in the hands of a few sellers. By these measures, the US oil industry is clearly at the competitive end of the spectrum. Table Four summarizes the concentration data on a top four-firm and top eight-firm basis for a number of the activities in which the firms in the US petroleum industry engage. The general conclusion is that on an across-the-board basis, economic activity in the US oil industry is absolutely unconcentrated, and relatively unconcentrated compared to many other sectors of the American economy. In general, the American economy can be characterized as effectively competitive. On the basis of concentration data, the US oil industry is not an exception to that rule. In fact, the concentration data are consistent with an assertion that the US oil industry is one of the more competitive of American industries.

Based on adjustments for regional markets and imports, the weighted average eight-firm concentration ratio for US manufacturing in 1966 was 60 percent.[16] This has been for decades a relatively stable number which is relevant today. With the exception of uranium

Table Four
Concentration in the US Oil and
Energy Industries, 1970

Activity	Top Four (Percent)	Top Eight (Percent)
Crude Oil Production [a]	27.1	43.0
Crude Oil and Natural Gas Liquids Reserves	35.5	58.5
Natural Gas Production [b]	24.4	39.1
Natural Gas Reserves [b]	30.0	47.1
Bituminous Coal Production	30.7	41.2
Uranium (U_3O_8) Production [c]	52.8	77.2
Gasoline Sales	30.7	55.0
Refining Capacity	33.3	58.7

Sources: Joseph P. Mulholland and Douglas W. Webbink, Federal Trade Commission Staff Report, *Concentration Levels and Trends in the Energy Sector of the US Economy* (Washington: Government Printing Office, 1974); Federal Trade Commission, *Preliminary Staff Report on Its Investigation of the Petroleum Industry,* Committee on Interior and Insular Affairs, US Senate (Washington: Government Printing Office, 1973); and Federal Energy Administration, *The Structure and Competitive Behavior of the Petroleum Industry, A Fact Sheet,* mimeo. (1975).

[a] Does not include royalty oil.

[b] Includes the United States and Canada.

[c] Adjusted to reflect U_3O_8 production of companies in addition to uranium milling companies.

16 W. G. Shepherd, *Market Power and Economic Welfare, An Introduction* (New York: Random House, 1970).

production, all of the eight-firm concentration ratios for oil and natural gas and coal production activities are less than the average for US manufacturing. Uranium mining and milling is a relatively new industry. Although the largest firm engaged in this industry is an oil company—Kerr-McGee Corporation—none of the eight largest uranium mining and milling companies in 1970 was one of the eight largest oil companies. Over the period 1955-70, there was considerable entry into uranium mining and milling, and concentration generally declined. If (1) the nuclear power industry is not aborted, (2) the demand for uranium mining and milling services grows, and (3) large oil companies are not prohibited by legislative fiat from entering this aspect of the energy industry,[17] it is likely that increased participation by large oil companies will reduce the level of concentration in uranium mining and milling to values consistent with the levels of concentration characteristic of other dimensions of the US oil and gas industry—that is, to effectively competitive levels which are near or below those levels of concentration typical of average US manufacturing industry.

Concentration, however, is a static measure. The efficiency of resource allocation involves a dynamic process. Over the period 1946-76, the US demand for petroleum products increased over 250 percent. Under these circumstances, one might expect considerable entry into the US refining industry. Part of the web of myth and error concerning the US oil industry is the mistaken allegation that there are substantial barriers to entry at all stages of the industry, and in particular to refining. The staff of the FTC states:[18]

> (T)he petroleum industry, and refining in particular, is also characterized by high barriers to entry . . . (with a) lack of substantial entry by new independent refiners over the last 20 years.

This allegation is typical of the quality of factual analysis characteristic of many industry critics. Table Five contains a record of the

---

17 There are horizontal disintegration proposals in the US Senate which would prohibit oil companies from participating in coal, uranium, or any aspects of the energy industries other than oil and natural gas. This is despite the facts that uranium is found in sedimentary basins about which oil companies possess considerable geological and geophysical knowledge, and that coal is a hydrocarbon about which oil company research laboratories have substantial expertise. Arbitrary prohibition of oil company participation in the development of these resources limits the range of talents available to help solve US energy supply problems.

18 Federal Trade Commission, *Preliminary Staff Report on Its Investigation of the Petroleum Industry*, p. 25.

Table Five
Refining Companies Whose Operating Crude Oil Distillation Capacities Grew to More Than 50,000 B/D Between January 1, 1951, and January 1, 1975

	Operating Refining Capacity [a]	
	on January 1, 1951	on January 1, 1975
Amerada Hess	— 0 —	730,000
Marathon Oil	31,000	324,000
Coastal States Gas	— 0 —	212,982
American Petrofina	19,800	200,000
Kerr-McGee	7,500	166,000
Commonwealth Oil Refining	— 0 —	161,000
Union Pacific (Champlin)	20,200	152,000
Murphy Oil	— 0 —	137,000
Koch Industries	— 0 —	109,800
Clark Oil & Refining	26,000	108,000
Tenneco	16,000	103,000
Crown Central	32,500	100,000
Toscopetro (The Oil Shale Corporation)	— 0 —	87,000
Charter	10,000	85,900
Agway	— 0 —	74,500
Farmland Industries	27,200	73,838
Tesoro Petroleum	— 0 —	64,000
Pennzoil	8,500	62,600
Apco Oil	10,000	58,670
Husky Oil	5,000	59,000
United Refining	5,500	58,000
National Cooperative Refining Association	20,000	54,150
Total of 22 Companies	239,200	3,181,440

Source: Statement of Walter R. Pierson, President of Amoco Oil Company, before the Subcommittee on Antitrust and Monopoly of the Senate Judiciary Committee, November 12, 1975.

[a] These capacities are as reported by the Bureau of Mines, except that they include the capacity of the Virgin Islands refinery of Amerada Hess on December 1, 1974, as reported by the Federal Energy Administration. The 1951 data are for the present firm or its lineal predecessor. A zero indicates that the company was not a refiner on January 1, 1951, and did not become a refiner by acquiring a company that was refining on January 1, 1951, although subsequent to its entry into refining it may have acquired such a firm.

entry and expansion of 22 companies into the refining industry serving US petroleum products markets.

Between January 1, 1951, and January 1, 1975, the 22 firms listed in Table Five expanded their capacity from 239,200 B/D to 3,181,-440 B/D. This is a net increase of 2,942,240 B/D. The expansion in refinery capacity of the 22 firms listed in Table Five represented approximately 33 percent of the total expansion in refinery capacity directly oriented toward the US market.

To put this expansion by the 22 smaller companies into more complete perspective, consider the growth of these companies in relation to Exxon—the largest US refiner. In 1951, Exxon refining capacity was over three times as large as the refining capacity of the 22 companies. In 1975, the refining capacity of the 22 firms was nearly three times as large as that of Exxon. Moreover, eight of the 22 companies were originally *de novo* entries into refining activity. These companies built or acquired over seven times as much US-directed refining capacity over the last quarter century as has Exxon.[19] These 22 firms now represent approximately 20 percent of total capacity—an increase from less than four percent in 1951.

All of this expansion by the 22 companies does not represent net additions to US-oriented refining capacity. Some of the growth of the 22 companies has been as a result of acquisition of existing capacity, rather than grassroots construction. If one were concerned only with contributions to growth in total US refining capacity, net additions to capacity would be the relevant measure. But in terms of the behavioral implications of the vertical foreclosure theories advanced by some industry critics,[20] any expansion in refining capacity by smaller firms is relevant. If smaller or less vertically integrated firms were being squeezed or foreclosed by larger or more vertically integrated firms, then *any* addition to refining capacity by the smaller firms would be surprising. It is of particular significance that not only have smaller firms entered, grown, and expanded in absolute terms, but the 22 firms in Table Five have increased in

19 These companies are not the only companies which have entered or expanded in refining. Refinery capacity figures by company are published according to various definitions by the US Bureau of Mines and the National Petroleum Refiners Association. We do not here attempt to reconcile reporting and statistical differences in these series. What is important is that any series on entry and expansion in refining tells the same basic story. Table Five and other data are indicative, however, of the quantitative significance of the participation of smaller companies in the growth of the US petroleum industry.

20 See, for example, the staff report of the Subcommittee on Antitrust and Monopoly of the Senate Judiciary Committee for the proposed legislation, S. 2387, The Petroleum Industry Competition Act.

relative size and importance. This is not simply a statistical illusion involving large percentage changes from a small base. The total fraction of capacity which these firms represent is substantial. One of the new entrants in Table Five—Amerada Hess—now operates the largest refinery in the world.[21]

In terms of both static and dynamic elements, the market structure of the US oil industry is consistent with effective competition. This corroborates the findings based on long-run retrospective profitability, and supports the contention that if the industry were not subject to regulatory and legislative uncertainties, and if the US price were rationalized relative to the world price, the adjustment process through which additional resources would be allocated to domestic energy production would be open and competitive. But despite the long-run structural and performance data, some observers question whether the behavior of the industry does not somehow manage to offset what would otherwise be judged to be a competitive result. Two areas of concern in this regard are joint bidding in offshore OCS lease sales and price formation in products markets. We now turn to these behavioral questions.

Behavior: Joint Bidding

It has been charged that joint bidding ventures in offshore lease sales are evidence of a collusive pattern in the petroleum industry which escapes the surveillance of the antitrust authorities.[22] This charge is inconsistent with the record of profitability for the industry (both for offshore activity and in aggregate) and the actual pattern of bidding behavior. The evidence is consistent with the proposition that the industry is in general effectively competitive—and particularly so with regard to offshore activity.

Joint bidding is a vehicle for pooling risks involved in offshore operations, and serves as a vehicle which enhances entry into offshore activity by relatively smaller firms. This opinion is consistent with an analysis of offshore lease sales by Professor Jesse W. Markham.[23] Markham found that there was no statistical evidence that joint bid-

---

21 The Caribbean refinery of Amerada Hess has a capacity of 700,000 B/D.

22 This section follows the discussion in E. W. Erickson and R. M. Spann, "The U.S. Petroleum Industry," in E. W. Erickson and L. Waverman, eds., *op. cit.*, vol. 2, *North America*, pp. 5-24.

23 Jesse W. Markham, "The Competitive Effect of Joint Bidding by Oil Companies for Offshore Leases," in Jesse W. Markham and Gustav F. Papanek, eds., *Industrial Organization and Economic Development* (Boston: Houghton Mifflin, 1970), pp. 116-135.

ding reduces the number of bidders, and that joint bidding is not inconsistent with an increase in the number of bidders and the average bid. This evidence is also consistent with a more detailed analysis of the actual bidding patterns and the rate of return on assets committed to offshore activity.[24]

The patterns for winning bids are summarized in Tables Six, Seven, and Eight. These tables show percentage bids in each category that were made by firms or groups of firms which contained no

Table Six
Joint Venture Bidding Patterns for Winning Bids, 1954-73 Sales

Number of Firms in Combine	Number of Bids	Percent Nonmajors
1	1121	49
2	356	24
3	145	43
4	206	46
5 and over	69	77
Overall	1897	44

[24]There have been a number of studies of the rate of return to offshore activity. These studies indicate that, in general, oil companies have earned rates of return to offshore activity which are consistent with effective competition. These studies include T. D. Barrow, "Economics of Offshore Development," *Exploration and Economics of the Petroleum Industry* (New York: Bender, 1967), vol. 5, pp. 133-146; A. R. Winzler, "Economics of Offshore Exploration—Post-Appraisal of Recent Sales," *ibid.*, vol. 7, pp. 69-89; Walter J. Mead, estimates contained in Nossaman, Waters, Scott, Krueger, and Riordan, *Study of Outer Continental Shelf Lands of the United States,* Public Land Law Commission, US Department of Commerce/National Bureau of Standards, revised 1969, pp. 521-527; US Department of the Interior, *The Role of Petroleum and Natural Gas from the Outer Continental Shelf in the National Supply of Petroleum and Natural Gas,* Bureau of Land Management, Technical Bulletin No. 5, May 1970; L. K. Weaver, H. F. Pierce, and C. J. Jirik, Offshore Petroleum Studies, *Composition of the Offshore US Petroleum Industry and Estimated Costs of Producing Petroleum in the Gulf of Mexico,* US Department of the Interior, Bureau of Mines, Information Circular 8557 (Washington: Government Printing Office, 1972); US Department of the Interior, *Rates of Return on the OCS,* Office of Program Coordination, May 7, 1975; Jesse W. Markham, "The Competitive Effects of Joint Bidding by Oil Companies for Offshore Lease Sales," *loc. cit.;* and E. W. Erickson and R. M. Spann, "An Analysis of the Competitive Effects of Joint Ventures in the Bidding for Tracts in OCS Offshore Lease Sales," in Hearings Before the Special Subcommittee on Integrated Oil Operations of the Senate Committee on the Interior and Insular Affairs, *Market Performance and Competition in the Petroleum Industry* (Washington: Government Printing Office, 1974), pp. 1691-1745. The numerical results of some of these studies suggest that oil companies in general have actually earned below normal rates of return to offshore activity. This is almost certainly true for some companies, but such a general interpretation should be treated with caution for two reasons. First, all of the studies depend to varying degrees on critical price and unit cost assumptions. This is, however, not unusual for any economic analysis of returns. Second, and more important, in the face of persistently low nominal returns, oil companies have continued to invest in offshore activity. The best interpretation of these studies is that there is a substantial body of evidence which unanimously supports the conclusion that in offshore activity oil companies have not in general earned rates of return in excess of the competitive, normal level.

60   *Oil, Divestiture and National Strategy*

Table Seven
Joint Venture Bidding Patterns for Winning Bids, 1972 Sales

Number of Firms in Combine	Number of Bids	Percent Nonmajors
1	63	60
2	52	27
3	39	41
4	24	25
5 and over	14	50
Overall	192	42

representatives of the eight major petroleum companies.[25] As Table Six indicates, approximately half of the winning bids were made by single firms or combinations of firms which included no representative of the eight majors. In addition, almost half of the single-firm winning bids were made by nonmajor firms. This evidence is not consistent with a situation in which the major firms are able to enforce collusive bidding arrangements as a result of their participation in joint bidding ventures.[26]

Tables Seven and Eight confirm the results of Table Six. In 1972, 42 percent of all winning bids were made by nonmajor firms, and 60 percent of winning single-firm bids were made by nonmajor firms. In 1973, 75 percent of all winning bids were made by nonmajor firms, and 36 percent of all winning single-firm bids were made by nonmajors. This is not evidence of collusive bidding patterns. When Tables Seven and Eight are combined and compared with Table Six, an interesting result emerges. In the combined 1972 and 1973 lease sales, 54 percent of all winning bids were made by single firms or combines which included no majors. This compares to the equivalent figure for all 1954-73 lease sales of 44 percent. Also, in the combined 1972-73 lease sales, 57 percent of all single-firm winning bids were made by nonmajor firms. This compares to the equivalent figure for 1954-73 lease sales of 49 percent.

---

25 As discussed above, "majors" are here defined as the eight respondents in *FTC vs Exxon*. A large number of firms are often designated as majors, but the focus here is restricted to those firms now under challenge by the antitrust authorities.

26 Nevertheless, the US Department of the Interior has recently issued regulations which prohibit the largest firms from bidding jointly with each other.

Table Eight
Joint Venture Bidding Patterns for Winning Bids, 1973 Sales

Number of Firms in Combine	Number of Bids	Percent Nonmajors
1	11	36
2	14	71
3	10	80
4	38	87
5 and over	31	74
Overall	104	75

These comparisons indicate that for a large number of firms, entry is possible into offshore activity; that joint bidding is not always necessary for such entry, but that it is a facilitating factor; and that entry has occurred over the 1954-73 period. (These conclusions are also supported by a similar analysis of second- and third-place bids.)

Out of a total of 776 joint ventures that submitted winning bids, only 91 (or 12 percent) consisted of majors alone. But 295 (or 38 percent) consisted of nonmajors only. One half of all joint ventures consisted of both majors and nonmajors, but the turnover in bidding partnerships was significant. There were no winning combines in excess of three firms which consisted only of majors. These data are a very strong indication that offshore activity is undertaken in a very competitive economic environment.

Behavior: Banked Costs

The prices which oil companies charge for refined petroleum products are constrained in two ways. First, the market limits the prices which firms realize for their output. Second, FEA price regulations establish ceilings above which firms may not set their prices.

The ceiling prices established by FEA regulations are firm-specific. Each firm has a set of ceiling prices on various products which are established as a function of base period prices and cost increases which the firm has experienced.[27] The ceiling prices are determined

---

27 The base period is May 1973. Increased crude oil costs are allocated to various products on the basis of the FEA refinery cost model. The cost allocation system has changed slightly from time to time, and now also includes some cost components other than crude oil. Under authority granted to it by Congress, but subject to Congressional review, FEA is gradually removing price controls on a product-by-product basis. At one time, however, all refined product prices were controlled.

on a month-by-month basis. The prices which firms can charge are
the lower of the two constraints—the market or the FEA ceiling. If
the market price is the ruling constraint, the firm is not passing
through into product prices and recovering all the cost increases which
FEA regulations allow. Under these circumstances, the firm is allowed
to "bank" costs. If a firm is banking costs, the market price is lower
than the maximum price—determined by base period price and allowable cost increases—which FEA regulations would permit the firm
to charge.[28] Banked costs can be saved and used by the firm in subsequent periods to relax the FEA price ceiling if it becomes the
ruling constraint.

The existence of dual market and FEA price constraints upon the
firm, the possibility of banking costs as a result of the market constraint being more binding than the FEA ceiling, and the fact that
firms did bank costs are an indication that refined products markets
in the United States are in general effectively competitive.

The pricing decision which firms make in effectively competitive
markets is different in kind from the pricing decision which firms
with market power make. Firms in effectively competitive markets
are price-takers. The prices at which they can sell their output are
determined by market forces. The prices of the various products which
the effectively competitive firm can produce and sell are established
by the general forces of supply and demand and are exogenous to the
firm. The competitive firm's decisions involve what mix of outputs
in what amounts to produce and offer to the market. Under these
circumstances, if competition causes market prices to be less than
the FEA price ceilings specific to any firm, that firm banks costs.

Firms with market power base their pricing decisions upon a more
complicated calculus. Rather than being price-takers at market-
determined price levels, firms with market power must take into
account the effect of the prices they set upon the amount demanded
of various products. The price responsiveness, or elasticity, of demand
is a critical element in their pricing decision. At higher prices, less
is demanded. Costs also go up or down as the amount produced varies
to meet demand at alternative prices. When a firm has market power

---

28 Cost banks are product-specific. FEA regulations allow switching among banks. For
example, cost increases allocated to middle distillates might be used by a firm to relax the FEA
price ceiling for gasoline if the market price is the ruling constraint for middle distillates and
the FEA ceiling is the ruling constraint for gasoline. The directions of permissable switching
among banks have varied from time to time. At the present time, the general pattern of
allowable switching is from all other products into gasoline.

and general pricing discretion, the pricing calculus is to take cost and demand conditions into account in order to find that price which maximizes the profits of the firm.

Under competitive conditions, when the firm is a price-taker, the firm offers a rate of output at which marginal costs are equal to price. Offering a rate of output at which marginal costs equal price is the profit-maximizing strategy for the firm, and it is in the firm's self-interest to do so. The equality of price and marginal cost is the critical determinant of an efficient allocation of resources. When a firm has market power, the profit-maximizing calculus of self-interest, together with the opportunities open to it, leads the firm to set a price in excess of marginal costs.[29] For a firm with market power, this can be expressed as

$$P = k \cdot MC$$

where the profit-maximizing price (P) exceeds marginal costs (MC) by the relative amount by which k, the factor which takes into account the price responsiveness of demand, exceeds unity.

This relationship has a very interesting implication. A profit-maximizing firm with market power always establishes prices which exceed marginal costs. Because k is a positive number which is greater than unity, a firm with market power which experiences an increase in marginal costs—say as a result of an increase in crude oil prices—will wish to increase prices by *greater* than the increase in marginal costs.[30]

The FEA product price control scheme relies upon base period prices and cost increases to establish ceiling prices. Since a firm with

---

29 The formal expression of this solution involves marginal costs (MC), the profit-maximizing price (P), and the elasticity of demand (η). When a firm with market power takes advantage of the price responsiveness of demand and maximizes profits, the relationship among these variables is

$$\text{(a)} \quad P = \frac{MC}{1 + \frac{1}{\eta}}$$

which can be reduced to

(b) $P = k \cdot MC$

where

$$\text{(c)} \quad k = \frac{1}{1 + \frac{1}{\eta}}$$

and is a positive number greater than unity because the elasticity of demand, η, which a firm with market power faces reflects the inverse relationship between price and quantity demanded, and is a negative number with an absolute value in excess of unity.

30 Consider a numerical example. If MC equals 5 and η equals -2, the desired profit maximizing price is 10. If MC increases by 5 units to 10, then if η remains at -2, the desired profit maximizing price is 20: MC has increased by 5 but desired price has increased by 10. Even if the elasticity of demand in this numerical example becomes more elastic as price rises so that η changes from -2 to -3, the FEA price constraint would bind a firm with market power.

market power which experienced an upward shift in marginal costs as a result of an increase in crude oil prices would desire to set a new profit-maximizing price which was proportionately greater than the increase in costs, firms with market power would tend to be bound by the cost-based FEA price constraint.[31] This means that firms with market power would be unlikely to bank costs because the prices they wished to charge would exceed the FEA price ceilings determined by their base period prices and cost increases.

Faced with increased costs and FEA cost-based price controls, the firms in the US petroleum industry banked costs. This means that in many cases the market was a more effective constraint than the FEA ceiling. Banking costs is behavior which is likely to be inconsistent with market power. Whatever their defects on other grounds, FEA price controls have given us another piece of evidence that the US oil industry is effectively competitive.

Conclusions

In terms of questions we set out to address, the answers are straightforward: (1) there is no monopoly power on the part of private companies in the domestic energy markets of the United States; that is, these markets are effectively competitive; and (2) market imperfections should therefore not affect our willingness to rationalize the world and the US energy price regimes. Nevertheless, we reveal a great reluctance in this regard. Part of this reluctance is buttressed by erroneous allegations of domestic energy monopoly. Part is a result of the natural and understandable unwillingness to pay higher energy prices, and the less reasonable apparent belief that by hiding our head in the sand the central realities of the energy situation will go away. And part is a result of an apparent willingness to incur substantial national security risks, high costs for synthetic and alternative fuels,[32] and subsequent adjustment costs rather than to allow oil companies to earn "windfall" profits as a result of taking

---

31 This is a general statement. As with most general statements, there are possible exceptions to it. There are certain combinations of cost and demand conditions (that is, where the elasticity of demand varies as price changes and marginal costs change as the rate of output varies) under which a firm with market power would find it worthwhile to bank costs. A formal statement of these conditions is not developed here, but the general conclusion holds. A firm with market power is less likely to bank costs than a price-taking firm in an effectively competitive market environment.

32 In terms of BTU equivalence, the break-even price for many alternative energy sources—ignoring the long lead times and relatively small contribution they can be expected immediately to make—is on the order of oil prices in the range of $25-$30 per barrel.

prompt and immediate steps to work ourselves out of the current slide towards greater and greater import dependence. In my opinion, the windfall profits issue, our failure to forge a prudent US energy policy, and our unwillingness to acknowledge the integrated major oil companies as principal social agents for the implementation of that policy all come back full circle to the erroneous allegations of domestic energy monopoly. Such charges are the dog in the manger of US energy policy.

Pretending the problem will go away, and distorting market signals with regard to the costs and benefits of domestic energy consumption and production, only increase our import dependence and raise the probability that the OPEC price will be higher rather than lower. With respect to "windfall" profits, one man's windfall is another's relief from regulatory inhibition. But the windfall profit issue is a political fact of life. It is also an economic fact of life that the major integrated oil companies are the principal social agents for increasing or maintaining oil and gas production in the United States—and perhaps coal and uranium production as well, if they are not prohibited from engaging in these activities. And it is abundantly clear from profitability and other data that there is a high social urgency for increased domestic energy supply investments. If a windfall profits tax is the political *sine qua non* for rationalization of the US and world energy price regimes, then such a pill should not be too bitter to swallow. But the realities of regulation-induced disequilibrium in US energy markets strongly suggests that any such tax should automatically phase out on a rapid schedule and be accompanied by a generous plowback provision. These are solvable policy problems. The mystery is why we seem so unable to make the appropriate adjustments. The nature of the world has changed, but the fault for our continued dilemma is *both* in our stars and in ourselves.

4

Divestiture and the World Oil Market

WILLIAM A. JOHNSON
RICHARD E. MESSICK

The United States Congress is now considering legislation that would require the separation of the major oil companies into producing, transporting, and refining-marketing firms.* At the moment, it appears that a principal justification for divestiture legislation is that it would weaken the OPEC cartel. Because the international oil companies are vertically integrated, many critics of the industry believe that the companies have several interests in common with the oil-producing nations and are, in effect, allies of these nations in their efforts to maintain oil prices far in excess of the costs of production. For example, Senator Philip Hart of Michigan, one of the principal sponsors of divestiture legislation, asserts that "the major oil companies are 'going along' with the OPEC cartel because it is in their corporate interests to."[1] Advocates of divestiture legislation contend

* Preparation of this essay was supported, in part, by a grant from the National Science Foundation and the Treasury Department. The views expressed here are those of the authors, and do not necessarily reflect the opinions of the NSF or the Treasury Department. The authors are indebted to a number of colleagues who read and commented upon earlier drafts of this paper. We would like to acknowledge particularly the valuable criticisms provided by Peter Trinkle of Exxon and Michael Cannes of the American Petroleum Institute. We remain, of course, responsible for any errors of omission or commission.

The authors are associated with the Energy Policy Research Project at George Washington University, Washington, D.C. A longer version of this essay will appear in the December 1976 issue of *Law and Policy in International Business*, the international law journal of the Georgetown University Law Center.
1 Press Release, Office of Senator Philip Hart, April 15, 1976.

66

that breaking up the companies will dissolve the community of interests between the international oil companies and the oil-producing countries. This, in turn, will make it much more difficult for these countries to sustain the current high world price for oil.

In this essay, we examine this argument in depth. In doing this, we discuss how the OPEC countries have managed to maintain relatively high prices; and how divestiture would affect OPEC's ability to function as an effective cartel, as well as the ability of the Arab producing countries to influence US foreign policy through the imposition of another oil embargo.

Is There a Community of Interests Between OPEC and the International Oil Companies?

The notion that the international oil companies and the oil-producing countries have a common set of interests, and that this explains the continued viability of OPEC as a cartel, appeared over a year ago in a report by the Senate Subcommittee on Multinational Corporations.[2] Subsequently, it has been adopted by the staff of the Senate Antitrust and Monopoly Subcommittee as a principal justification for vertical divestiture legislation.[3] Anthony Sampson, a British investigative journalist, has popularized it in his best-selling book on the international oil companies, articles in the popular press, and testimony before Congress.[4]

According to this argument, OPEC faces two basic problems as a cartel. The first is to keep prices up by developing a system for allocat-

---

2 US Senate, Committee on Foreign Relations, Subcommittee on Multinational Corporations, *Multinational Oil Corporations and US Foreign Policy*, 93rd Congress, 2d Session, January 1975, pp. 10-13. The staff of the Senate Antitrust and Monopoly Subcommittee also cites Professor Morris Adelman's analysis of the world market as justification for divestiture. (See, for example, US Senate, Committee on Foreign Relations, Subcommittee on Multinational Corporations, Prepared Statement of Morris Adelman, *Hearings on Multinational Corporations and United States Foreign Policy*, 94th Congress, 1st Session, pt. 11, 1975.) In a recent article, however, Adelman has rejected current divestiture proposals. M. A. Adelman, "Splitting the Oil Companies Won't Help," *Washington Post*, May 1, 1976, p. A14.

3 Senate Antitrust and Monopoly Subcommittee, Majority Staff, *Vertical Divestiture in the Petroleum Industry*, undated, pp. 13-15; see also *Hearings on the Petroleum Industry before the Subcommittee on Antitrust and Monopoly of the Senate Judiciary Committee*, 94th Congress, 1st Session, pt. 1, November 1975.

4 Anthony Sampson, *The Seven Sisters, The Great Oil Companies and the World They Shaped* (New York: Viking Press, 1975), pp. 299-307; Anthony Sampson, "How the Oil Companies Help the Arabs Keep Prices High," *New York Magazine*, September 22, 1975; Anthony Sampson, "US Oil Companies: Accomplices of OPEC?" *Washington Post*, November 11, 1975, p. A14; "Seven Sisters Author Talks of Big Oil," Interview with Anthony Sampson, *Washington Star-News*, November 3, 1975, p. 1; Anthony Sampson, Statement before the Subcommittee on Antitrust and Monopoly of the Senate Judiciary Committee, February 3, 1976. See also, Paul Lewis, "Is It Time to Sob For the Seven Sisters? Not Yet," *New York Times*, September 21, 1975, Section IV, p. 4.

ing production among its members in a way that balances world oil supply with demand. But because experience shows that this is an inherently divisive task for the members of a cartel to undertake themselves, OPEC would be much more likely to continue as an effective cartel if a third party were to do the actual production prorationing for it.

OPEC's other problem is to insure continued outlets for its members' oil. Because no OPEC member's national oil company is capable of marketing all of its crude oil at present, OPEC must depend on foreign firms to distribute its oil in the consuming countries. On the other hand, OPEC members do not want to sell to just any firm. There is a danger that aggressive buyers of crude, seeking the lowest price, would trigger a price war among OPEC members by playing one country off against the other. Thus, OPEC seeks to deal only with those companies that have little or no interest in lower prices and are willing to establish long-term relationships under which they become tied to particular member countries.

Thus, the interests of the international oil companies, it is argued, mesh perfectly with the needs of OPEC. Each international oil company operates in more than one country. And, because each company wishes to protect its interests in the countries in which it operates, it balances its production in such a way that no country is so dissatisfied with production rates that it will sever its ties with the company. The net effect of this system, as all the companies simultaneously balance their liftings, is that production is allocated more or less equitably among OPEC members. This is done without the necessity of OPEC members having to face up to the potentially divisive issue of agreeing on output levels among themselves.

OPEC's problem of finding buyers who are willing to sign long-term contracts, and who at the same time are reluctant to try to bargain down crude prices, is also solved by dealing with the international companies. Because each company wants long-term supply guarantees to insure that its refineries will operate at full capacity, each is willing to enter into long-term purchase agreements with individual countries. Furthermore, the companies will not try to bid down prices because they have sizeable oil reserves outside OPEC that increase in value whenever OPEC raises its price. Hence, the companies also benefit from OPEC's successes as a cartel.

Perhaps the best way to analyze this argument is to begin by reviewing the nature of oil company-host government relationships. Originally, a company or consortium of companies negotiated a concession agreement with a country that gave it the exclusive right to all oil discovered in the concession area. In return, the government usually received an advance payment, and royalties based on production rates. But the producing countries eventually became dissatisfied with these concession agreements. Beginning in 1968, OPEC members asked for a revision of the concession contracts. In September 1971, OPEC met in Beirut and passed Resolution 139 calling for the achievement of "effective participation" in the assets of the producing companies by OPEC members. Under the participation agreements negotiated subsequent to the Beirut Resolution, the countries received a share of the oil produced in their territory. During this period, the companies and the countries, as joint owners of oil concessions, had a common interest in price and production levels. But this did not last for long.

The producing countries found during 1974, after the Arab oil embargo ended, that the companies were reluctant to buy back country-owned or "participation" oil because its price was substantially higher than the cost of company-owned or "equity" oil. In September 1974, OPEC met in Vienna to resolve the problem. Although the results of this meeting were inconclusive, the problem was gradually solved during the Fall and Winter of 1974 by the actions of individual OPEC members. For example, Kuwait negotiated a new agreement with BP and Gulf raising the royalty rate on equity oil from 14½ to 16⅔ percent and increasing the income tax from 55 to 65.76 percent. Because this did not completely eliminate the gap between equity and participation prices, Kuwait also required the companies to increase their liftings of participation oil from 350,000/bpd. to 450,000/bpd. Similar changes in the royalty rates, income tax rates, and liftings requirements were imposed on the companies by other producing countries. The effect was to increase incentives for the companies to lift participation oil.[5] It accomplished this, however, by reducing substantially any advantage the companies realized from their remaining equity positions. The net result was that the common interest between the companies and the countries in price and output levels was largely

---

5 *Oil and Gas Journal*, September 1974, p. 108. See also, William A. Johnson, "Trends in World Oil Prices and Production," unpublished paper, George Washington University, Energy Policy Research Project, October 8, 1974.

dissolved. Today, the primary interest of the companies lies in buying crude as cheaply as possible in order to be in a better competitive position downstream.

Moreover, by 1976, most OPEC countries had either fully nationalized, or were about to nationalize, oil company properties within their borders. (See Table One.) This is true of OPEC's most important

Table One
Producing Country Shares in the Ownership
of Oil Industry Assets
June 1976

Country	Government Participation Rate	Comments
Saudi Arabia	60	60 percent participation since 1974. Discussions for 100 percent takeover of ARAMCO's holdings nearing completion. Effective date of nationalization retroactive to January 1, 1976.
Iran	100	Nationalization in 1951.
Iraq	100	Almost total nationalization since 1973.
Kuwait	60;100	Gulf-BP holdings totally nationalized in March 1976; 60 percent participation for other foreign companies, although their properties are to be nationalized soon.
United Arab Emirates	60	100 percent takeover under consideration.
Qatar	60	100 percent takeover is imminent.
Libya	51;100	BP, Bunker, Hunt, Amoseas, ARCO, and Shell's share of OASIS group totally nationalized; government owns a 51 percent share of Occidental and remainder of OASIS holdings.

Algeria	100	Nationalization of all but Getty, CFP, and ERAP production since 1971, or approximately 80 percent of total.
Nigeria	55	55 percent participation in production of oil since 1974. Nigerian government has subsequently announced that it will assume complete ownership and control as soon as sufficient skilled local manpower is available.
Gabon	25	Although government participation is limited, Gabon has insisted on other stringent concessions from the oil companies.
Venezuela	100	Total nationalization in early 1976.
Ecuador	25	All petroleum is the property of the state; 25 percent of Texaco/ Gulf's operations taken over in 1974, and government now plans to go to 51 percent.
Indonesia	100	Nationalization between 1963 and 1968.

Source: Federal Energy Administration, *The Relationship of Oil Companies and Foreign Governments* (Washington: US Government Printing Office, 1975), supplemented by discussions with various government and oil company officials.

members—Iran, Iraq, Kuwait, Libya, Venezuela, and Saudi Arabia. Only Ecuador, Gabon, and Nigeria, all minor producers, seem content to allow the companies to retain significant equity holdings, at least for the time being.

As a result, the companies are now acting essentially as service contractors, producing oil and maintaining the logistical systems necessary to sustain production in the individual countries. For this, the companies are paid a fee of 22 cents a barrel. Proponents of divestiture believe this fee perpetuates the common interest of the companies and the countries. Thus, for example:[6]

---

[6] Memorandum from Walter S. Measday to Charles Bangert, both of the Senate Antitrust and Monopoly Subcommittee, "Companies Affected by Proposed Divestiture Legislation," March 30, 1976, p. 2.

While (the 22-cent fee) is low compared to their historic profit, it is quite high by any other standard and is nothing they would want to lose. Moreover, this special relationship enables the companies to remain as marketers of OPEC crude despite nationalization. In effect, it enables them to preserve their vertical integration even after losing their equity interest in OPEC production.

There are several flaws in this reasoning. First, the margins allowed the oil companies by several OPEC countries are much lower than 22 cents per barrel. In Venezuela, the latest tax law changes will allow a margin of only 19 cents.[7] In Iran, the effective margin, according to a representative of the Iranian Consortium (the group of companies that has produced and marketed Iranian oil since 1954), is now about 12 cents. The 22-cent margin is a theoretical norm more honored in the breach than in practice.

Moreover, a 22-cent margin is low when compared to the profits the companies can make on production outside OPEC. For example, despite the fact that "new" oil prices have been rolled back under the Energy Policy and Conservation Act, oil companies are realizing a substantially greater profit on production of "new" oil in the United States. In some instances, the profits are measured in dollars, not cents.

If, in fact, the margin allowed on production in OPEC countries is attractive, one would expect the companies to be increasing their investment in exploration and development in OPEC relative to other areas of the world. This pattern of investment did, in fact, exist prior to 1971, when OPEC first began to exercise its newly discovered power over the oil companies, and production in the OPEC countries was highly profitable. At that time, the US, Canadian, and European shares of total company investment in exploration and production were falling steadily each year, while the shares of the other non-Communist countries, primarily the OPEC countries, were rising. (See Table Two.) Since 1971, however, this trend has been reversed. OPEC's share of total investment has fallen, while the non-OPEC share has increased year after year. In short, OPEC's squeeze on company profits has had the effect one might anticipate. Rather than the oil companies' continuing to tie their futures to the producing countries, there has been

7 *Petroleum Intelligence Weekly*, April 12, 1976, p. 3.

Table Two
Share of Investment in Exploration and Production
in Non-Communist Countries
1967 through 1974 (Percentage of Total)

Year	United States	United States, Canada, and Europe	Rest of the Non-Communist World (Primarily OPEC)
1967	64	80	20
1968	64	77	23
1969	61	76	24
1970	58	75	25
1971	48	67	33
1972	57	74	26
1973	57	76	24
1974	58	77	23

Source: Computed from Chase Manhattan Bank, Energy Economics Division, *Capital Investments of the World Petroleum Industry,* 1968 through 1975.

a noticeable shift in investment in exploration and development from OPEC to the United States and other non-OPEC countries.

In other words, the international oil companies appear to be shopping around for crude oil in at least one important way—through their exploration and development programs. Before the international oil companies can produce crude oil outside OPEC, they must first explore for and develop it. Unfortunately, this takes time—perhaps as long as a decade—to accomplish.

It is also argued that the companies want to continue as service contractors in the various producing countries to assure access to limited crude supplies. As a result, the companies are balancing off production curtailments in these countries and, in this way, prorationing production for the OPEC countries. It is correct that the companies are anxious to have assured supplies of crude oil. No refiner relishes uncertainty over the supply of its principal raw material. Mobil, for example, is seeking to expand its share of Saudi crude oil, and to become involved with the Saudi government in the development of various downstream activities.[8] But Mobil's motivation stems from a conviction that Saudi Arabia is where much of the world's future crude

8 See Mobil's 1975 *Annual Report.*

oil supply will be found; and whether we like it or not, the world will have to depend heavily on Saudi Arabia for its future needs. Mobil may well be correct. If it is, there is probably relatively little that the US government can do to limit demand for Saudi oil. The problem lies, however, with the uneven generosity of nature rather than integration of the oil companies.

Even so, does this special relationship really guarantee a market for Saudi Arabia's crude oil? The answer is no. Mobil is no more guaranteeing a market for Saudi crude than the New York Stock Exchange is guaranteeing a market for Mobil's stock. Rather, the consuming nations of the world are assuring the market for Saudi oil. As long as the consuming countries demand energy, and are unable or unwilling to find less expensive alternative sources, Saudi Arabia—and other members of OPEC, for that matter—will be able to sell their oil at whatever price the market will bear.

Some critics of vertical integration believe that the companies are indifferent to price increases by OPEC. The companies own sizeable reserves outside OPEC, and the value of these reserves increases each time OPEC raises prices. Thus, it is argued, the companies and the countries have a common interest in higher oil prices.

Before analyzing this argument, it must be sharpened considerably. A price increase for crude oil will—other things being equal—cause sales of refined products to decline. This, in turn, will result in a reduction in profits on a company's refining and marketing operations, because the fixed costs of these operations will be spread over a smaller sales volume. Hence, only if the gain from an increase in the value of the company's reserves offsets the loss on marketing and refining will higher oil prices be in a company's corporate interest.

Suppose some companies have made this calculation and have concluded that price increases are to their advantage. We would expect these companies to encourage price increases by the producing countries by increasing output in those countries that are price leaders. Or, at the least, we would expect the companies with an interest in higher prices not to discourage price increases by reducing output in those countries that do raise prices. Yet, unless there is industry-wide collusion, this would not occur. All companies compete in the same product markets, and any company not buying crude at the lowest possible price will be at a competitive disadvantage in these markets. We are not aware of any serious allegations of an industry-wide conspiracy to keep oil prices high. Furthermore, if there were such a conspiracy, it would be readily apparent by examining publicly available data on oil prices and liftings. Oil liftings in those countries with high prices would increase while those in countries with low prices would decrease. This pattern of production has not occurred, particularly since OPEC's October 1974 changes in price formulas.

In February 1975, Libya cut its prices to make its crude oil more competitive. Several days later, Abu Dhabi also cut prices to bolster sagging markets. In both countries, the companies had not been lifting the amounts of crude oil that had been expected, largely because Libya had placed an unrealistic transportation cost premium and Abu Dhabi an unrealistic quality premium on their oils.[9] In March 1975, Algeria cut its crude price slightly to bring it into line with the price of Arabian light. In April 1975, both Libya and Abu Dhabi again reduced their crude oil prices in an attempt to reverse a steady decline in output.[10] Abu Dhabi's price cut was reported to be a concession to the companies for using their "best efforts" to reach the government's production target for the year.[11] On June 1, Libya again cut the price of its crude oil in order to give the companies an incentive for further liftings. Meanwhile, Indonesia was holding its prices firm and, as a result, was losing markets.[12]

Nigeria also reduced its prices during the first two quarters of 1975, but not by enough to increase company liftings. According to *Petroleum Intelligence Weekly,* the "only customers really seeking Nigerian crude are US companies that don't seem to care that the oil is 'overpriced' . . . Apparently, the workings of the US government's cost equalization program and the availability of low cost domestic oil makes this possible."[13] In other words, the US government's price and allocation controls appear to have encouraged the very actions of the oil companies which vertical divestiture legislation is supposed to correct.

Several of the OPEC countries have, in effect, reduced their prices

9 *Petroleum Intelligence Weekly,* February 10, 1975, pp. 3-4; and February 17, 1975, pp. 5-6. For a more thorough discussion of price cutting practices by the various OPEC members in late 1974 and early 1975, see Ray Vicker, "Some Oil-Producing States Shave Prices, But No General Reductions Are Expected," *Wall Street Journal,* January 29, 1975, p. 28; and James Tanner and James Carberry, "As An OPEC Summit Nears, Price Shaving is More Widespread," *ibid.,* February 28, 1975, p. 1.
10 *Petroleum Intelligence Weekly,* March 10, 1975, p. 1; March 31, 1975, p. 6; and April 21, 1975, pp. 1-3.
11 *Ibid.,* April 21, 1975, p. 3.
12 *Ibid.,* May 5, 1975, p. 6; May 26, 1975, p. 7; and June 16,1975, pp. 1-2.
13 *Ibid.,* July 14, 1975, p. 1; and July 7, 1975, pp. 5-6.

by providing more favorable credit terms and various under-the-table price reductions. By July 1975, price shaving among certain OPEC countries had become so widespread that Algeria was driven to criticize publicly "unjustified" price cuts by Nigeria, Iraq, and Libya.[14] At the beginning of 1975, Libya had been producing at about 38 percent of its capacity; by year's end, it had raised its production for the fourth quarter of 1975 to 72 percent of capacity, largely because of its price shaving. A fall-off in Nigerian production was also slowed primarily because of that country's price cuts.[15]

By the Fall of 1975, it was Kuwait's and Saudi Arabia's turn. Pressures began to mount on Persian Gulf crudes, with some price erosion in spot markets. In November, both Kuwait and Saudi Arabia shaved the official sales prices of their heavy crude by a modest ten cents a barrel in order to align them with the prices of their light crude oil.[16] Kuwait's reduction in the price of heavy oil, although extremely modest, was bitterly critized by Iraq.[17] This, in turn, worsened a potentially explosive problem in the Persian Gulf region because of Iraq's claims on Kuwait as an integral part of its own territory.

In early 1976, Iran began to feel the effect of Kuwait's and Saudi Arabia's cut in the price of heavy oil.[18] Iran had also expected a ten percent increase in the prices of both its heavy and light crude oils as a result of OPEC's December 1975 decision to increase the price of Saudi Arabian marker crude by ten percent. Saudi Arabia and several other OPEC countries increased the price of their heavier crudes by a smaller amount, however, with the result that Iranian heavy crude could not compete and company liftings fell.

The oil companies have begun buying elsewhere. The Iranian government alleges that the Consortium has violated a contractual obligation to produce a specified minimum amount of oil. The Consortium denies that it ever made such a commitment. In effect, if Iran is to set the price of oil, then the companies must reserve the right to determine how much they will buy. In February, Iran was forced to pare the price of its heavy oils by 9.5 cents. According to the oil companies, however, this was not enough to bring Iranian heavy crude prices into

---

14 *Ibid.*, May 26, 1975, pp. 1-2; and July 14, 1975, p. 3.
15 *Ibid.*, July 21, 1975, pp. 1-2; and August 4, 1975, p. 1. See also, Table Five.
16 *Ibid.*, October 27, 1975, pp. 1-2; and November 17, 1975, pp. 1-2.
17 See "Kuwait Price Cut Stirs New OPEC Controversy," *Oil and Gas Journal*, November 24, 1975, p. 21.
18 *Petroleum Intelligence Weekly*, January 26, 1976, pp. 1-2.

line with prices charged by other countries in the region.[19] The Consortium continues to resist Iranian government efforts to force increased liftings of heavy crude oil.

There is concern among some members of the Consortium that the pressure on Iran to lower its prices may actually be eased by the United States government. There is support, particularly in the State Department, for US actions to stabilize Iranian prices and production at relatively high levels. This might be accomplished by US government purchases from Iran for storage under provisions of the Energy Policy and Conservation Act of 1975. There have also been reports that US suppliers of military hardware are being encouraged by Washington to accept hard-to-sell Iranian heavy oil as payment for aircraft, with the oil to be purchased, in turn, by the US government for strategic storage.[20]

Support for US efforts to maintain Iranian oil revenues is rooted in the belief that Iran, because it is non-Arab, will continue to supply oil to the United States regardless of developments in the Arab-Israeli conflict. Iran is also thought essential to the maintenance of US interests in the region. Without Iran, the United States might have to place a substantial military capability in the Persian Gulf. There is, in other words, a shared interest between the United States and Iran. The US government, by helping to maintain a strong and friendly Iran, is also helping to assure stability in the Persian Gulf and to prevent disruption of US oil supplies obtained from the area.[21] This may or may not prove to be the right policy. If it is, it involves a cost to the United States and other consuming countries in the form of higher prices for oil. But to allege that the companies are at fault for not applying sufficient pressure on Iran misses the mark. The problem is not shared interests between the companies and Iran, but shared interests between the US government and Iran.

In passing, it is worth noting that at least once before, the structure of the world oil market and the relationship between the companies and the OPEC countries was believed to be the key to OPEC's survival. No less an authority than Sheik Zaki Yamani, the Saudi Petro-

---

19 *Ibid.*, February 16, 1976, pp. 5-6.

20 For example, see *ibid.*, April 5, 1976, pp. 1-2; and *Wall Street Journal*, May 12, 1976, p. 8.

21 This is, of course, not the first time that the US government has been concerned with the amount of oil lifted in and revenues paid to Iran. After the Shah's return to power in Iran, the State Department made sure that oil liftings were increased. See, for example, *Multinational Oil Corporations and US Foreign Policy*, Chapter 3.

leum Minister, predicted that if the taxation system in effect in the
late 1960s and early 1970s were changed, and the companies' holdings in the OPEC countries nationalized, oil prices would "collapse."[22]
The taxation system has been changed and nationalization has occurred; but OPEC has not collapsed.

In short, the internationals have shifted from one source of crude
to another in response to changes in price. Other analysts have also
noted this pattern of behavior.[23] Shopping around suggests that the
companies are no longer making production decisions solely or even
largely with an eye toward protecting their residual interests in particular producing countries.

In summary, we have seen that the companies no longer have an
equity position in the majority of OPEC countries. They have become,
instead, service contractors lifting oil for a fee that is insufficient by
itself to keep the companies tied to OPEC over the long run. Furthermore, we have argued that it is not the oil companies but the consuming
nations that are guaranteeing a market for OPEC's oil. Finally, we
have shown that the companies are clearly responding to price incentives in programming production levels in each country, and that
they do not have an interest in higher crude prices. Hence, the notion
that the structure of the world oil market has created a community
of interest between the international companies and the oil-producing
countries is incorrect.

How Does OPEC Succeed As A Cartel?

If the companies are not maintaining the cartel, what makes OPEC
work in the absence of a formal plan for prorationing? The answer is
that OPEC is a managed cartel, or what economists sometimes call a
"structured oligopoly." A few countries have been willing to assume
most of the production curtailments necessary to maintain an artificially
high price for oil. Most important has been Saudi Arabia. The periodic
price increases by OPEC have, in fact, been increases in the price of
Saudi Arabian light crude oil, or what has come to be known as
"benchmark" or "marker" crude. In effect, OPEC meets periodically
to persuade the Saudis to raise the price of their benchmark crude.
The other OPEC countries, at least in theory, are supposed to raise

22 Cited in M. A. Adelman, "Is the Oil Shortage Real? Oil Companies as OPEC Tax-
Collectors," *Foreign Policy*, Winter 1972-73, p. 88.
23 See, for example, Douglas Bohi and Milton Russell, *US Energy Policy: Alternatives for
Security* (Baltimore: Johns Hopkins University Press, 1975), p. 60.

the prices of their oils by like amounts. Many have not, however, or if they have, have shaved the prices of their crude oil by various means, such as lower transportation and quality differentials.

Those countries that have an interest in maximizing production of crude oil have been able to do so under the system established by OPEC simply by adjusting the prices of their crude oil by a small amount relative to Saudi marker crude. What makes the system work is, essentially, the willingness of Saudi Arabia, and certain other

Table Three
Capacity and Production for Various
Producing Countries

	Mid-1975 Capacity	1975 Production	Production as a Percent of Capacity
	(Million Barrels per Day)		
Saudi Arabia	11.50	7.08	62
Kuwait	3.50	2.08	59
Libya	2.50	1.52	61
Iraq	3.00	2.25	75
UAE	2.34	1.69	72
Algeria	1.00	0.92	92
Qatar	0.70	0.44	63
Egypt	0.35	0.25	71
Syria	0.20	0.16	80
Total OAPEC*	25.09	16.39	65
Iran	6.80	6.07	89
Venezuela	3.00	2.35	78
Nigeria	2.50	1.78	71
Indonesia	1.70	1.31	77
Gabon	0.25	0.21	84
Ecuador	0.25	0.17	68
Total OPEC**	39.04	27.87	71

*Excludes Bahrain.
**Includes all OAPEC countries except Bahrain, Egypt, and Syria.
Source: Treasury Department.

member countries, to accept lower levels of output to maintain the cartel price.

The effect on liftings of crude oil is evident in data assembled in Table Three. In 1975, OPEC as a whole produced at 70 percent of its estimated capacity. Saudi Arabia produced at 62 percent, however, while Kuwait, Libya, and Qatar produced at 59, 61, and 63 percent, respectively. All other OPEC countries achieved much higher levels of capacity utilization. Interestingly, those countries that have a need for additional foreign exchange, and therefore an interest in higher liftings of crude oil, have operated at the highest rates of capacity utilization. Algeria produced at 92 percent of its capacity; Iran at 89 percent.[24] On the other hand, those countries that have little need for additional foreign exchange have shown the greatest inclination to allow reductions in their rates of utilization. Saudi Arabia, Kuwait, Libya, and Qatar, together, absorbed about 60 percent of OPEC's excess capacity in 1975.

The division between the various OPEC countries becomes even starker when one examines changes in capacity utilization during 1975. (See Tables Four and Five.) In both the first half and fourth quarter of 1975, capacity utilization was 68 percent for all OPEC countries. During the first six months of the year, about half of OPEC's members operated at or below 68 percent of capacity. During the fourth quarter, only three OPEC countries fell below the OPEC average: Saudi Arabia, Kuwait, and—by a small amount—Venezuela. By contrast, all other OPEC countries had substantially higher rates of capacity utilization.

Of all OPEC members, Venezuela has probably been the most stubborn in its refusal to cut prices. Venezuela has also imposed some of the most stringent taxes on the oil companies, and as a result, has lost its share of the market to other members of the cartel.[25] Venezuela has good reason to do this. Its conventional oil reserves are in absolute decline for want of new discoveries. Unlike most other members of OPEC, its reserves are now projected to last only a little more than a decade at current rates of production. For this reason, Venezuela has sought to extend the life of its revenues by lowering output. At the

---

24 Production at between 90 and 95 percent of capacity is the maximum feasible for any country. This allows for adverse weather, transportation bottlenecks, well maintenance, earthquakes, and other natural phenomena, all of which have slowed or halted operations in the various producing countries at one time or another.

25 *Petroleum Intelligence Weekly*, December 29, 1975, p. 1; and January 5, 1976, pp. 3-4.

Table Four
Production as a Percentage of Capacity for
Various Producing Countries
First Half 1975

	Production (Million Barrels per Day)	As a Percentage of Capacity
Saudi Arabia	6.82	59
Kuwait	2.13	61
Libya	1.14	46
Iraq	2.18	73
UAE	1.49	60
Algeria	0.93	93
Qatar	0.45	64
Egypt	0.24	69
Syria	0.15	75
Total OAPEC*	15.53	62
Iran	5.43	80
Venezuela	2.53	84
Nigeria	1.71	68
Indonesia	1.24	72
Gabon	0.21	84
Ecuador	0.14	56
Total OPEC**	26.40	68

*Excludes Bahrain.
**Includes all OAPEC countries except Bahrain, Egypt, and Syria.
Source: Treasury Department.

same time, it has tried to maximize revenues by setting prices and taxes as high as possible. Iran's capacity utilization also declined significantly by the fourth quarter of 1975. Iran, like Venezuela, has been relatively intransigent on prices, at least until the first quarter of 1976 when, because of reduced liftings by the oil companies, it made a small 9.5-cent cut in the price of its heavy oils.

Capacity utilization for all other OPEC members either remained the same or increased throughout 1975. Especially noteworthy were

Oil, Divestiture and National Strategy

Table Five
Production as a Percentage of Capacity for
Various Producing Countries
First Quarter 1975

	Production (Million Barrels per Day)	As a Percentage of Capacity
Saudi Arabia	6.80	59
Kuwait	1.82	52
Libya	1.80	72
Iraq	2.23	74
UAE	1.87	78
Algeria	0.93	93
Qatar	0.52	74
Egypt	0.27	78
Syria	0.18	92
Total OAPEC*	16.42	65
Iran	4.86	72
Venezuela	2.02	67
Nigeria	1.95	78
Indonesia	1.40	82
Gabon	0.20	81
Ecuador	0.18	73
Total OPEC**	26.58	68

*Excludes Bahrain.
**Includes all OAPEC countries except Bahrain, Egypt, and Syria.
Source: Treasury Department.

sharp rises in production as a percentage of capacity for those countries most active in price-cutting during the year. This was particularly true of Libya, Abu Dhabi, Qatar, and Nigeria.

In Kuwait and Saudi Arabia, however, capacity utilization was significantly lower during the fourth quarter of 1975. Together, Kuwait and Saudi Arabia accounted for 54 percent of OPEC's underutilized capacity during the last three months of 1975. Why? Both countries are limited in their ability to spend the foreign exchange earned from additional sales of oil. Additional foreign exchange earnings simply add to their petrodollar accumulations, and will be invested—for the most part—in bank deposits and short-term securities in Europe and the United States, a use of funds not assigned a particularly high priority by either country.

By early 1976, some Kuwaiti officials began to question that country's policy of shutting in oil production, partly because of concern about possible deterioration in the long-run value of oil, and perhaps more important, because of the loss of associated natural gas production needed to fuel the Kuwaiti economy. Some increase in output to about two to 2.2 million barrels per day now seems likely, possibly through price shaving. If so, barring any significant change in total demand for oil, Saudi Arabia would be left to absorb most of OPEC's surplus productive capability on its own.

The Saudi role is not especially unique. Several observers have noted that small nations often fail to pull their own weight in a common effort, leaving to the larger countries a disproportionate share of the costs of making an alliance work.[26] Over the long run, OPEC will most likely continue to be Saudi Arabia's special burden. Mabro states: "Allowing for necessary compromises made for the sake of solidarity within OPEC, it is fair to say that the price of oil is as high as Saudi Arabia is prepared to let it be."[27] Mabro also notes that Saudi Arabia is not restricting output to maintain prices. Rather, Saudi Arabia is prepared to sell substantially higher amounts of oil at the price determined by OPEC.

This is where many critics of the international oil companies have gone wrong. Because classical cartel theory holds that output must be restricted to maintain price, the critics have searched for a prorationing mechanism. Realizing that the countries themselves are not programming output, they have seized on the idea that the companies are doing it for them.[28] In fact, OPEC sets the price for Saudi marker crude. Other OPEC countries then adjust the prices for their own crude oils to reflect differences in transportation costs and quality and, if they wish, to stimulate production at high levels.

Transportation charges and quality premium fluctuate significantly

---

26 For example, see Mancur Olson, Jr., and Richard Zeckhauser, "An Economic Theory of Alliances," *Review of Economics and Statistics,* August 1966, pp. 266-279.

27 Robert Mabro, "OPEC After the Revolution," *Millenium* (London School of Economics), Winter 1975-76, p. 192.

28 "OPEC, like any cartel, . . . must agree on how the members apportion the necessary production cutback among themselves. . . . Even during its recent high point, it has been unable to reach agreement. It has, however, found a substitute . . . decision(s) have been left to the international companies." *Vertical Divestiture in the Petroleum Industry,* p. 14.

over time. For this reason, there is a continual search for the correct price, that is, the price that accurately reflects the actual quality and transportation differentials between a country's oil and Saudi benchmark crude. Because prices are continually changing at the margin, as some countries set their price too high and others too low, attention is focused on making marginal adjustments to price, rather than the infinitely more difficult and potentially divisive task of setting output levels for each of the cartel's members. OPEC's members are aware of the danger of production prorationing. The minutes of the OPEC meeting of September 1974 show that the countries, for the most part, refused to discuss output restrictions, fearing "a dangerous race of price cuts as every producer tries to maintain his share in a limited market."[29]

Saudi Arabia's unique position in OPEC as the only country that must maintain the price for its benchmark crude gives it awesome power over the other members of the cartel. Mabro states:[30]

> The only course of action open to Saudi Arabia if she wishes to regain control over the volume of her exports is to vary the marker price. But this is tantamount to dissolving OPEC. After all, the only significant function of the organization at present is to fix the reference price . . . Saudi Arabia is the linchpin of OPEC. One could almost say without too much exaggeration that OPEC is Saudi Arabia.

How long will Saudi Arabia continue to bear most of OPEC's burden? Probably as long as Saudi Arabia is unable to absorb all of the revenues it earns or will earn from its production of oil through its domestic development programs and assistance to other countries. Because production is declining or has peaked in most of the other OPEC countries, and also in such non-OPEC countries as the United States and Canada, the demand for Saudi oil will almost certainly increase, not decrease, over the next decade. The likelihood that Saudi Arabia will be compelled by its need for foreign exchange to undermine or destroy the system that sustains OPEC is very low indeed.

This appears to be borne out by the fact that, during the first quarter of 1976, Saudi production rose by over a million barrels per

---

29 Cited in Louis Kraar, "OPEC is Starting to Feel the Pressure," *Fortune*, May 1975, p. 187.
30 Mabro, *loc. cit.*, p. 196.

day. This reflects, to some extent, Saudi Arabia's failure to increase
the prices of its other crude oils by the ten percent increase in the price
of its marker crude, as decreed by OPEC in December 1975.[31] The
major reason, however, was revival of demand for oil in Europe, and
an increase in consumption and fall in production in the United States.
Both trends should continue, and both will work against any efforts
by the consuming nations to apply pressures on Saudi Arabia to
increase output in order to lower prices. In short, OPEC is here to
stay as a viable, effective cartel for a long time to come. It does not
prorate production among its members because it does not have to.

It should be clear from how OPEC has functioned that the equity
and other interests of the oil companies in producing countries have
had very little to do with the pattern of prorationing established through
the price mechanism by the OPEC countries. The oil companies have
had no equity position in Algeria and Iran for years. Yet their liftings
from Algeria and, until recently, Iran have been fairly high. Until
1976, they had substantial equity positions in Saudi Arabia and
Kuwait. Yet their liftings of Saudi and Kuwaiti oil have been relatively
low. In fact, the international oil companies have been shopping around
for crude oil, increasing liftings from those countries willing to shave
prices in order to maximize output and to satisfy their foreign exchange
needs. By contrast, those countries that have ample foreign exchange
earnings have been less willing to shave prices; for this reason, the
companies have had less incentive to purchase their crude oil. Price
is the prorationing mechanism that has been adopted by OPEC, and
as long as Saudi Arabia is willing to play the game, OPEC will remain
intact.

Even granting this, critics have still faulted the international oil
companies for not having made massive shifts in demand from one
producing country to another in response to the limited price competition that has occurred. This, they conclude, must reflect the
special relationships between the international oil companies and the
producing countries. As we have shown, the companies have shifted
liftings to a degree. But the ability of the companies to make major
changes in oil suppliers is limited by technology, at least in the short
run. Because refineries are set up to operate on a particular type of
crude oil, substitution of one type for another is restricted.

More important, because Saudi Arabia has been willing to hold the

---

31 See *Quarterly Economic Review: Saudi Arabia, Jordan,* no. 1–1976 (London: Economist Intelligence Unit, 1976), p. 3.

line on the price of its marker crude, price adjustments by the other OPEC countries have been modest. There has been no reason for the other OPEC countries to make substantial reductions in prices to assure sales of oil at desired levels. And because the other OPEC countries have not made major cuts in their own crude oil prices, there have been no major incentives to the companies to make massive shifts in their sources of supply. Are the companies to be blamed? We would think, rather, that it is the structure of the OPEC cartel and, above all, the fact that only one country can break OPEC as an effective cartel in the near future. That country, Saudi Arabia, has neither the intention nor the incentive to do so.

What Would Be the Impact of Vertical Divestiture on the World Oil Market?

What is likely to occur if the proponents of vertical divestiture succeed? Will divestiture result in lower oil prices? The experience of the consuming nations in 1973-74 can hardly be encouraging. When, in October 1973, the Arab nations imposed their oil embargo, several companies panicked. In December 1973, an auction in Iran netted prices in excess of $17 per barrel.[32] Several days later, an auction yielded $22.60 per barrel for Nigerian crude.[33] These auction prices encouraged OPEC to raise the price of Saudi marker crude twofold. In each case, the major reason the companies bid excessive prices was panic. Significantly, those refiners bidding extraordinary prices were, without exception, independents lacking substantial amounts of their own crude oil.

Parenthetically, some of these same companies walked away from purchase agreements calling for extraordinarily high prices after the US government established its crude oil allocation program early in 1974. Why should a crude-short refiner buy Iranian oil at $17 per barrel when the US government was providing it at $7 per barrel? Because many independents defaulted on agreements with the producing countries during this period, some of these countries now have little or no desire to enter into future supply arrangements with independent oil companies. This fact is often seized upon by proponents of divestiture as one more indication of the community of interests

---

[32] *Petroleum Intelligence Weekly,* December 17, 1973, pp. 1-2.
[33] *Ibid.,* December 31, 1973, p. 5.

that exists between the producing countries and the integrated oil companies.[34]

Would the break-up of the integrated oil companies weaken OPEC? This is not very probable. What, in fact, seems likely is that it would, by definition, result in the proliferation of crude-short refineries which, during the next embargo or supply shortage, may also engage in panic bidding in an effort to assure continued access to their principal raw material. Whether the existence of a standby allocation program or a "more equitable" distribution of crude oil supplies would lessen this panic buying remains to be seen.

It is particularly difficult to justify the divestiture of domestic US refining and marketing from domestic production if the primary objective of the Congress is to reduce ties between the international oil companies and the producing countries. If anything, the retention of integration in the domestic industry, while eliminating whatever equity position may still remain in foreign producing countries, should encourage maximum development of US productive capability at the expense of the OPEC countries. This has, in fact, been recognized by Anthony Sampson, one of the more vocal critics of the international oil companies, in testimony before the Senate Antitrust and Monopoly Subcommittee.[35]

Divestiture would almost certainly put the United States in a weaker position relative to other consuming nations. We have argued elsewhere that, if a divestiture law were passed, at least some integrated companies would be likely to move their headquarters abroad and focus on foreign operations.[36] These newly created foreign integrated oil companies would then be competing in the world oil market with weaker, nonintegrated US companies. The foreign companies would almost certainly be in a better position to obtain crude if another supply interruption should occur.

Once again, the experience during the last embargo is instructive. In October 1973, the Arab countries totally curtailed oil shipments to the United States, as well as to Canada and countries in the Caribbean

---

34 For example, see the comments by Charles Bangert, General Counsel of the Senate Antitrust and Monopoly Subcommittee, *Hearings on the Petroleum Industry before the Subcommittee on Antitrust and Monopoly of the Senate Judiciary Committee*, 94th Congress, 1st Session, Part 1, November 1975, pp. 376-377.

35 Anthony Sampson, Statement before the Subcommittee on Antitrust and Monopoly of the Senate Judiciary Committee, February 3, 1976, p. 13.

36 William Johnson, Richard Messick, Samuel Van Vactor, and Frank Wyant, *Competition in the Oil Industry* (Washington: George Washington University Energy Policy Research Project, 1976), pp. 50-51.

which have historically shipped large amounts of refined products to
the United States. Most Arab producers also embargoed the Netherlands and a few other countries in Europe whose policies were not
sufficiently supportive of Arab interests. All other countries were to
continue to receive Arab oil; and a few, including France, Spain, and
the United Kingdom, were to receive all the Arab oil they needed.

But it is now clear that the Arabs' intentions were frustrated. The
primary reason for this was the action of the international oil companies. The companies followed a policy of "equal suffering." All
countries, whether embargoed or not, were to share more or less
equally in the crude oil that was available. This was accomplished
through the mechanism of swapping. For example, Iranian oil des-
tined for France could be diverted by the companies to the United
States. Meanwhile, Saudi oil that would have been shipped to the
United States in the absence of the embargo was shipped instead to
France.

There is now general agreement that the companies managed to
share the shortages remarkably well under the circumstances. According to a report by the Senate Subcommittee on Multinational
Corporations:[37]

> The US international oil companies individually decided that
> each would attempt to meet the requirements of the embargoed
> nations while strictly complying with the Arab directives. Essen-
> tially, US companies decided that "the pain should be evenly
> spread" to all major consuming regions—that the reduction in
> supplies should not be "targeted" against individual countries.
> This decision was taken at the highest corporate levels . . .
>
> Once the allocation base had been established, each company
> sought to distribute supplies as evenly as possible to consuming
> nations. Thus, a supply cutback of ten percent would ideally
> result in each consuming nation receiving 90 percent of its base
> demand. Actual supply redistribution, however, was hampered
> by a variety of political, economic, technical, and legal factors.
> In addition to Arab destination restrictions, several consuming
> nations imposed restrictions which hampered transshipments as
> well as re-exportation of petroleum imported solely for refining
> on export account.

---

37 *Multinational Oil Corporations and US Foreign Policy*, p. 147.

The Federal Energy Administration, in assessing the embargo experience, concluded that "it is difficult to imagine that any allocation plan would have achieved a more equitable allocation of reduced supplies."[38] Robert Stobaugh also found that shortages were equalized in all countries, with no one country experiencing significantly greater shortages than the others.[39] The European Economic Community released a report in December 1975 which reached similar conclusions.[40]

What motivated the international oil companies to ship more oil to the embargoed countries than the Arabs intended or historic patterns of distribution would have dictated? One reason was a desire to minimize frictions with the various consuming countries that would otherwise experience disproportionate shortages. The policy of equal suffering was least likely to result in adverse reactions by these countries against the oil companies. Perhaps more important, however, was the fact that the international oil companies have major investments in refining and marketing in precisely those countries that were totally embargoed, particularly in the United States. The policy of equal suffering, in effect, allowed more crude oil to flow to the companies' downstream investments, and in this way minimized potential financial hardships of the embargo. Put differently, because of the vertical integration of the international oil companies, the companies actually had a shared interest with the United States that served to dampen the impact of the embargo on the US public. At the beginning of the 1973 Arab-Israeli War, the US Treasury Department estimated that a fully effective embargo would deprive the United States of about 2.8 million barrels of oil per day out of a total consumption of 16 million barrels. In fact, the US shortfall was about half this amount. This was due, very largely, to the oil companies' policy of equal suffering.

What would happen in the event of another embargo, if the international oil companies were prohibited by a divestiture law from owning significant downstream investments in the United States? Clearly, they would have less incentive to follow a policy of equal sharing of oil shortages. Especially if these companies reincorporated as European

---

38 US Senate, Committee on Foreign Relations, Subcommittee on Multinational Corporations, *US Oil Companies and the Arab Oil Embargo: The International Allocation of Constricted Supplies,* a report prepared by the Federal Energy Administration's Office of International Energy Affairs, 94th Congress, 1st Session, January 27, 1975.

39 Robert B. Stobaugh, "The Oil Companies in the Crisis," *Daedalus,* Fall 1975, pp. 179-202. See especially, pp. 198-199.

40 Commission of the European Communities, *Report by the Commission on the Behavior of the Oil Companies in the Community During the Period from October 1973 to March 1974* (Brussels: December 1975), pp. 57-75.

firms, the result could well be far greater susceptibility to pressures by those countries not targeted by the Arabs. Several foreign governments have actually concluded from the embargo experience that their oil companies must integrate upstream into the world petroleum market, rather than continue to rely heavily upon US-based international oil companies for crude oil. For example, the Japanese Ministry of International Trade and Industry recently announced plans for "streamlining" Japanese oil companies in order to develop integrated operations ranging from the development of oil resources to the sale of final products.[41] Various European countries have also established state oil companies intended to challenge the domination of US-based integrated oil companies in the producing countries.

The disintegration of the US internationals could also weaken the International Energy Agency and undermine the solidarity of the consuming nations. The European countries and Japan were willing to join the IEA oil-sharing plan partly because of their concern that five of the seven sisters were US firms. This, they thought, gave the United States a potentially advantageous position relative to other consuming countries. One way to assure that the US-based internationals do not discriminate against Europe and Japan in the event of another supply shortage would be to formalize oil-sharing programs under the IEA umbrella. This has now been accomplished in Chapter III of the Agreement on an International Energy Program, initialed by the 17 nations that are members of the IEA.

What would happen in the event of another embargo, if the United States unilaterally dissolved its special relationship with the international oil companies? What would happen, in particular, if these companies changed their home base from the United States to Europe or Japan? Europe and Japan would have much less incentive to remain in the oil-sharing plan, and might even set in motion procedures for terminating their participation. This would, in turn, make the next embargo far more effective. The Arab producing countries would then be able to pinpoint another embargo against their intended victim, the United States, and would have less reason for concern that the embargo was hurting other consuming countries that have generally been supportive of Arab interests. With the IEA sharing plan dissolved and the US-based oil companies destroyed, the United States would be in a highly exposed position in the event of another embargo.

---

41 *Japan Economic Journal*, January 20, 1976, p. 6.

By putting the United States in such a position, the Congress would actually become an ally of the Arab producing states in their struggle with Israel. The purpose of the 1973-74 embargo was to force the United States to moderate its support for the state of Israel. This objective was largely frustrated as a result of the oil companies' ability to spread the effects of the embargo among all consuming countries. Under divestiture, the companies would no longer have the incentive and capability of doing this. Ironically, despite its repeated displays of support for the Israeli cause, the US Congress, through its advocacy of divestiture, would actually further the interests of Israel's enemies.

5

The Soviet Union as a World Oil Power

MARSHALL I. GOLDMAN

As with so many other decisions in the world today, American policy regarding the oil industry must take developments in the Soviet Union into consideration. This was not always so. Indeed, until recently few people have paid much attention to the Soviet Union as a petroleum power. But by 1975, the Soviet Union had become the world's largest producer, and the third largest exporter of petroleum (after Saudi Arabia and Iran).

It is true that the Soviet Union is also the world's second largest consumer of petroleum, and therefore may soon find that its domestic needs have outstripped productive facilities. But this day may not be as close as some people think, in view of the fact that the Soviet Union has large oil deposits and apparently has not fully exploited them. One analyst has calculated that the Soviet Union and China together have produced only nine percent of their potential oil recovery capacity, while the United States has already extracted about 45 percent.[1] American policymakers should be aware of recent developments in the Soviet petroleum industry, its present capabilities, and the options open to the Soviet Union in the years ahead.

---

[1] J. D. Moody and R. W. Esser, Mobil Oil Corporation, "An Estimate of the World's Recoverable Crude Oil Resources," Ninth World Petroleum Congress, Tokyo, 1975, p. 19.

Russia as a Petroleum Exporter

The fact that the Soviet Union is an exporter of petroleum should not come as a surprise to those who know Russian history. Prior to the Russian Revolution and the discovery of the large fields in the Middle East, Russia was one of the world's largest exporters of crude oil. Western-controlled firms were set up in Baku and were a major factor in world markets. To be sure, world demand was not very large at the time, but the historical antecedent of Russia as a major world petroleum trader is there.

After the revolution, the oil fields were nationalized. Nevertheless, in view of its own relatively modest domestic needs, it made sense and hard currency for the Soviet Union to keep up its exports. There were periodic disruptions for political reasons (and sometimes for military reasons), but the Soviets kept exporting. From the late 1940s to the mid-1950s, the bulk of their exports, however, were diverted to their allies in Eastern Europe and China. In the years following Stalin's death, the Soviets tried gradually to re-enter Western markets—in order to reclaim their old market share, as Soviet authorities sometimes put it. They were fiercely resisted by Western governments and oil companies. In addition to the desire to hold down competition, there were fears that Western governments and consumers would become overly dependent on the Soviet Union, which in turn would make those who bought from the Soviet Union politically and possibly militarily vulnerable.

There were also economic considerations. The Russians were attempting to enter an already well-supplied market, and price-cutting seemed to be the only way to do so. Consequently, their offerings often had destabilizing effects on the market. By the late 1950s, the downward pressure on prices became distressing to several of the oil-producing countries; and they were especially disturbed because their expectations had only recently been stimulated by the increase in petroleum prices set off by the closing of the Suez Canal in 1956. But these higher prices had fallen again once the Canal was reopened and normal supplies started to flow from the Middle East. Prices were further affected by the competitive impact of the Soviet offerings. Ultimately, the Soviets found a taker in the person of Enrico Mattei of Italy and his maverick state-owned corporation, ENI. In an effort to halt any further erosion in prices, and eventually to increase prices, several oil-producing states organized the Organization of Petroleum

Exporting Countries (OPEC) in September 1960. The Soviet Union
was thus a major factor in provoking that action.

Soviet petroleum exports, including sales to the West, have grown
continually in virtually every year except 1964 and 1974. The average
annual growth was 14 percent from 1956 to 1975, or about a 13-fold
increase. At one point, Italy imported over 22 percent of its petroleum
from the Soviet Union.[2] Later this was reduced to about 10 percent, but
smaller countries like Finland and Iceland depended on the Soviet
Union for as much as 80 percent and 65 percent, respectively, of their oil.

Soviet Consumption

It was not only petroleum exports that increased, of course.
Petroleum output also rose sharply. Total production increased from
83.8 million tons in 1956 to 491 million tons in 1975, or by six
times, about 9.8 percent a year. As an indicator of just how much
exports and output have grown, it is perhaps useful to point out that
1975 exports of 130 millions tons (which constituted over 26 percent
of total production) exceeded the total volume of production in 1959.
(And even then, the Soviet Union exported 25 million tons, or 20
percent of total output.)

Recently, there have been signs that the rate of growth of Soviet
petroleum output may be slowing down. According to the Tenth
Five-Year Plan, 1976-80, petroleum output is slated to grow only
5.2 to 5.9 percent per year. This would be a decline from the 6.8
percent annual growth rate achieved in 1971-75. Even so, if the
Soviet Union achieves its goal for 1980, this would still be a substantial accomplishment, inasmuch as almost every other large producer in the world (except Iraq) has been cutting total output, and
not just the rate of growth.

The question remains, however, as to what this decline in the rate
of growth will mean for Soviet exports to the West, especially in view
of what appears to be an increasingly absorbent market at home. Will
the Soviets be able to continue to set aside about 26 percent of
their output for export, as they are presently doing? Domestic needs
are growing in the Soviet Union; and if unrestrained, will grow faster
than production. For example, while Soviet automobile output in

---

2 Marshall I. Goldman, "The Soviet Union—The Oil Crisis: In Perspective," *Daedalus*, Fall
1975, p. 130.

1970 was only 344,000 units, by 1975 (with the completion of the Fiat-built plant) production had soared to 1.2 million units. How can the Soviets increase exports and still cater to this growing internal demand?

Despite the fact that, in recent years, domestic net consumption of oil frequently rose somewhat faster than output, there is strong evidence that the Soviet Union can, if necessary, control consumption. Like other countries, the Soviet Union has begun to have second thoughts about de-emphasizing coal production. As a result, coal is one of the few commodities whose production is slated to increase faster in the Tenth Five-Year Plan period than during the Ninth Five-Year Plan. In addition, as taut as the Soviet economy often appears to be, there nonetheless seems to be room for further tightening. Whereas domestic consumption of petroleum was growing at about seven percent a year until 1975, in that year net consumption increased by less than five percent. In view of the fact that most of the rest of the world has been reducing actual physical consumption of petroleum, this indicates that the Soviet Union can cut even more before the exporting surplus is affected.

Still, there are uncertainties. Will the Soviet Union be able to increase its output, and will it be able to avoid diverting its exportable petroleum to the East Europeans, whose needs are also growing? These are not easy questions to answer. So far, Soviet planners project a continuing increase in production during the Tenth Five-Year Plan, even though the rate is due to diminish. Yet a major portion of the future increase in output is scheduled to come from remote areas of Siberia and from offshore fields. This will require sophisticated drilling and shipping technology, most of which the Soviet Union seems to lack. Whether or not the Soviet Union is able to exploit these resources depends in large part on its ability to purchase and utilize foreign technology.

The governments which control this technology face a dilemma. If they provide the Soviet Union with it, the increased output of petroleum will undoubtedly strengthen the Soviet Union both domestically and internationally. At the same time, to the extent that the Soviet Union chooses or finds it necessary to sell this petroleum in the West, the amount of available oil is increased and the West is thereby strengthened as well.

Eastern Europe

Of course, the Soviet Union may find itself faced with irresistible demands for oil from Eastern Europe. Until recently, Soviet economic policy was in fact designed to make the East Europeans dependent on the Soviet Union for an important proportion of their raw materials, including petroleum. But that policy has now been drastically revised. Sensing the opportunities ahead, Soviet officials as early as the mid-1960s began urging the East Europeans to seek elsewhere for raw materials, and in particular for oil.[3] The Soviets stressed that the sale of raw materials to Eastern Europe often cost the Soviet Union more than the rubles it received in payment. Implicit in all this was the calculation of the opportunity cost of lost sales to the West, where they could earn hard currency for their oil. These lost sales became even more tempting as raw materials, and particularly petroleum prices, began to rise in 1973, especially during the Arab oil embargo.

The effect of this on Eastern Europe has been sharp and painful. At one time, several East European countries imported practically all of their oil from the Soviet Union. Gradually, however, the East Europeans have begun to reduce their dependence on the Soviets. Between 1959 and 1973, the East Germans reduced the share of Soviet oil in their total consumption from 94 to 80 percent. (The percentage rose to 87 percent in 1974.) The Czechs, who as late as 1969 were wholly dependent on the Soviet Union for crude oil, now manage to obtain at least a small percentage outside the bloc. Hungary and Czechoslovakia are cooperating with Yugoslavia in building a pipeline from the Yugoslav coast inland to Czechoslovakia and Hungary. This pipeline will probably be fed with oil from Kuwait and Libya, which are respectively putting up $125 million and $70 million to help finance construction.

To prod the East Europeans in their search for alternatives, the Soviet Union unilaterally raised the price of its oil to the East Europeans by about 130 percent in January 1975. In view of the fact that throughout the Arab oil embargo and into 1974, the Soviet Union did not raise its prices to Eastern Europe, one would have supposed

3 G. Prokhorov, "Mirovaia sistema sotsializma i osvobodivshiesia strany," *Voprosy ekonomika,* November 1965, pp. 84-85; O. Bogomolov, "Khoziaistvennye reform i ekonomicheskoe sotrudnichestvo sotsialisticheskikh stran," *ibid.,* February 1966, pp. 85-86; M. Sladkovskii, "XXII s'ezd KPSS i problemy ekonomicheskogo sotrudnichestva sotsialisticheskikh stran," *ibid.,* April 1966, p. 96; N. Volkov, "Struktura vziamnoi torgovli stran SEV," *Vneshniaia torgovlia,* December 1966, pp. 10-12; *Foreign Trade* (USSR), June 1973, p. 14.

that the East Europeans would not have had too much to complain about. From their perspective, however, the price increase was a shock. The original contract had stipulated that prices would remain fixed until January 1976. Further, when the prices were last established in January 1971, the East Europeans were paying the Soviet Union a relatively higher price than West European purchasers of Soviet petroleum. Finally, the Soviet Union increased prices on petroleum and other raw materials more than the Eastern Europeans were allowed to raise their prices on the industrial goods they sold in return to the Soviet Union.

The consequences of the Soviet price rise have farreaching implications. Countries like Hungary, which once had substantial favorable trade balances with the Soviet Union, now find that they have an unfavorable balance. This, in turn, has stimulated them not only to look for other sources of petroleum, but to find other ways of reducing their economic dependence on the Soviet Union. The difficulty is that many of the alternative petroleum sources in the Middle East require hard currency and at present charge even higher prices than the Soviet Union. The Soviet price for petroleum is now based on a moving average of world petroleum prices over the preceding five years. Because the average still encompasses prices for years prior to the price rise in 1973, the Soviet price is still below the present world price. Consequently, the East Europeans have been scrambling to work out foreign aid and barter deals with the Middle East countries, with repayments in petroleum to be paid later.

Another approach has been to seek petroleum substitutes. Unfortunately, this is not an attractive option, except for Poland and Rumania. The only other fuel available to most of the East Europeans is lignite, which is a dirty and not very efficient fuel. Lignite also causes high levels of air pollution in Eastern Europe, especially in the Winter when homes burn it for heat. Much of the sharp increase in petroleum consumption in Eastern Europe was due to the desire to reduce pollution levels, which meant less emphasis on lignite. Now this may have to be reversed.

The effect of these developments has been a sharp decline in the yearly increase of petroleum sold to Eastern Europe. Whereas prior to the embargo, sales of Soviet petroleum to Eastern Europe were rising at about ten to 12 percent a year, in 1974 and 1975 the increase was only six to seven percent. Poland, like many Western countries,

98

6 Oil, Divestiture and National Strategy

actually reduced its petroleum consumption. In 1973, Poland imported
14.2 million tons of crude oil and petroleum products, while in 1974
it imported only 13.6 million tons. Almost 500,000 tons of that
600,000-ton drop was the result of a reduction in imports from the
Soviet Union.

Hard Currency Possibilities

Restraining the flow of oil to Eastern Europe, and the parallel
conservation of petroleum at home, have positioned the Soviet Union
to increase its exports of petroleum to the hard currency world. Since
petroleum is the Soviet Union's largest hard currency earner, this is
no minor matter. Despite the fact that the Soviet Union is the world's
largest producer and exporter of machinery, very little of it is sold
or accepted in hard currency markets. Because the quality and service
of Soviet equipment is often so poor, most customers have been in
the developing nations or Eastern Europe, neither of which disposes
of hard currency. Consequently, $5 billion of the Soviet Union's $6.7
billion of hard currency exports in 1974 were in the form of raw
materials; and petroleum accounted for almost 40 percent of the
Soviet Union's total hard currency earnings from exports.

The fact that the Soviet Union earned so much from petroleum is
not as surprising as it might sound. Since the Soviet Union is the
world's third largest exporter of petroleum, it should be earning large
sums even if only 30 percent of its oil exports go to hard currency
purchasers. This windfall was particularly important in 1973 and 1974.
In the latter year, the Soviet Union had an overall hard currency trade
surplus of almost $600 million, which was one of the largest it ever
had. But as some of the OPEC members also discovered, what looked
like a long-term surplus turned out to be short-lived. The fourfold
increase in oil prices to the West first set off an inflation, and then a
recession. (In contrast to its restraint in Eastern Europe, the Soviet
Union joined the OPEC countries in raising the price of petroleum
sold to the West.) The Soviet Union, like OPEC, prospered during
the inflation. They also suffered during the recession. Much to everyone's surprise, the demand for petroleum was not as inelastic as had
been assumed. Consumption fell; but at first, the oil-producing countries did not cut back on their expectations. Like Iran, Indonesia, and
Nigeria, the Soviets developed visions of boundless bounty, and set
off on major purchasing sprees. By the time deliveries were made to

the Soviet Union in 1975, prices on many goods turned out to be higher than expected, as inflation began to work its way through the price system. Import bills of the oil-producing countries soared, while export earnings remained relatively constant. Petroleum earnings barely increased, and in some cases fell. The situation was especially acute for the USSR because the demand for its other raw material exports was even more income-elastic than in the case of petroleum. Demand and prices for such products as timber and metals fell off radically. The effect was inevitable. While in 1974 the Soviet Union had one of the largest trade surpluses in its history, 1975 brought the reverse—a record $3.6 billion deficit. The recession explained the bulk of the shortfall, although the 1975 crop failure cost the Soviet Union another $1.1 billion in the United States alone.

In order to work its way out of this deficit, the Soviet Union apparently has decided to rely in large part on increased petroleum exports. This is reflected in the spectacular jump in total petroleum exports in 1975 over 1974, as shown in the table. Soviet exports rose by 14 million tons, of which seven million went to the hard currency countries. This was after a slight drop in total exports in 1974. Despite the reduction in the quantity of petroleum exports that year, higher prices mean that export earnings from petroleum in 1974 were double the preceding year, and increased to $2.6 billion.

The reason for the Soviet decision to concentrate on petroleum exports is easy to understand. Despite the weakening of the market in 1975, the Soviet Union still has less difficulty in fighting its way into hard currency petroleum markets than into other markets. Western companies no longer refuse to refine or market Soviet oil. Indeed, Western buyers are now quite receptive because Soviet oil

Soviet Oil Production and Exports
(Million Tons)

Output		Exports		
		Total	CMEA	Hard Currency
1972	394	107	57	34
1973	421	118	63	36
1974	451	116	67	31
1975	491	130	72	38

increases their supply alternatives. In sum, not only is there a hard currency market for Soviet petroleum, but the Soviet Union wants to sell to this market; and for the time being, at least, it has the surplus output to offer to hard currency customers.

Political Implications

From what we have seen, it seems reasonable to argue that the Soviet Union will continue to play a role—and probably an increasing one—in Western markets. What are the risks and benefits for the West? Clearly, the fact that the Soviet Union has a relatively large quantity of petroleum to sell in hard currency markets gives it a strong lever; and Moscow has not hesitated to use its trade for political purposes when it thought it convenient to do so.

The most blatant use of Soviet oil as a political weapon took place in October 1956. In order to punish Israel for its invasion of the Sinai, the Russians withheld oil exports that had already been contracted for, and never resumed shipments to Israel.[4] The amount involved was relatively small, but the step was taken solely for political reasons. The Soviets exercised much the same kind of economic and political pressure on Yugoslavia from mid-1949 to 1956, during which period Soviet petroleum supplies were cut off completely in an effort to punish Tito. Similarly, the Soviets reduced their exports to China in mid-1964 as tensions between the Soviet Union and China intensified.

Whether or not the Soviet Union could or would adopt such measures today is hard to predict. To be effective, Moscow would have to select countries that were heavily dependent on the Soviet Union for their supplies. Except for Eastern Europe, there are not many other countries where this is the case. Such tactics might work in Finland and Iceland, but probably not elsewhere; even Italy has reduced its relative dependence on the Soviet Union. If anything, recent trends seem to point in the opposite direction. Given the lure of precious hard currency earnings, the Soviet Union seems to be doing everything it can to prove that it is a dependable supplier of petroleum. In the short run, at least, this has been from purely economic motives. The profit drive has caused the Soviet Union to overlook not only ideology (which for the cynical among us is not particularly shocking), but also political advantage, which is a much more sacred cow.

---

4 Samuel Pisar, *Coexistence in Commerce* (New York: McGraw-Hill, 1970), p. 275.

An example of how Soviet economic opportunism triumphed over politics and ideology occurred during the Yom Kippur War oil embargo. On the one hand, the Soviet government urged the Arabs to adopt and to continue the embargo of oil shipments to the West; but on the other, it did everything it could to take advantage of the profit opportunities created by the embargo.[5] While praising the Arabs for their refusal to sell to the United States and the Netherlands, the Soviets simultaneously availed themselves of the profits to be earned by exporting to the very countries that were embargoed by the Arabs. In the case of the Netherlands, the Soviet Union increased its exports by about one million tons, and in the process earned over $130 million more than in the nonembargo year of 1972. In the United States, Soviet sales jumped from $7 million in 1972 to $76 million in 1973, primarily in the fourth quarter.

When Arab spokesmen criticized the Soviet Union for its two-faced policy, the Soviets defended themselves by denying any violation of the embargo. But while it is true that the Soviet Union never formally agreed to adhere to the embargo, Moscow certainly supported it with outspoken rhetoric. The Soviets also maintained that they were following the spirit of the embargo, and that they were not taking any petroleum from the Arab countries and transshipping it to the embargoed West. Their purchases, the Soviets insisted, would only be consumed in the USSR or in other Communist countries.[6] In actual fact, however, according to some Western traders, the Soviet Union did try to sell Middle East petroleum to the embargoed countries. Again, the attraction of profit in the West outweighed the unpleasantness of enmity in the East.

Similarly, the Soviets have not held back because of ideology. The Soviets are rapidly moving into Western markets, not only through the sale of petroleum to Western firms, but by the formation of Soviet-owned multinational corporations. In both Belgium and Great Britain, the Soviets are either the sole or majority owner of a concern called Nafta. Nafta (GB) is primarily a wholesaler and retailer. It imports Soviet petroleum, and then either sells it to Western oil companies or retails it directly through franchised and wholly-owned filling stations. At one time, there were as many as 150 Nafta (GB) filling stations in England. While some of the stations have since

---

5 See Goldman, *loc. cit.*
6 *Soviet News,* December 4, 1973, p. 508; *New Times,* November 1973, p. 22.

been closed, Nafta (GB) is again engaged in expanding the network by increasing both the number and the size of its stations.

The operation in Belgium is even more ambitious. Nafta (B) owns a modern tank farm with a capacity of about 850,000 tons in the Antwerp harbor. It, too, sells to other oil companies. It also operates a network of 23 filling stations, which it is trying to expand. The Soviet Union has also bought and built a large tanker fleet, the purpose of which is ultimately to free the Soviet Union from the fear of a possible embargo on the shipment of goods to and from the USSR that might some day be imposed by Western ship owners. For a time, Nafta was also active in trying to build and then buy a refinery near its tank farm in Antwerp. They were effectively frustrated, however, by other oil refiners and the Belgian government. In the early 1970s, the Soviets even tried to build a refinery in the United States. From all reports, both Nafta (GB) and Nafta (B) are efficient and profitable, and—like all multinationals—profits are sent back to headquarters, not in New York or London, but in Moscow. Again, the not-so-subtle motive is profit and hard currency.

In Nafta (B), the Soviet Union is creating a fully integrated multinational firm. It has its own sources of supply, its own tankers and pipelines, its own tank farm, its own wholesale operations, and its own filling stations. Moreover, it is in the process of consolidating and expanding the system.

Natural Gas

While the main focus of this essay has been on petroleum, it is important at least to mention natural gas. Although not as critical an energy source as oil, gas does play a vital role in some parts of Western Europe. The Soviet Union is the world's largest producer of natural gas after the United States, and soon will be the world's largest exporter. Moreover, since gas consumers are for the most part tied to their pipelines, it is difficult to switch suppliers. Once plugged in, it is usually costly if not impossible to make a change.

The Soviet Union's role in natural gas markets has evolved gradually. Initially, it exported only to its neighbors in Czechoslovakia and Poland. In 1967, Soviet exports began to reach outside the bloc to Austria. The Soviet Union also began to import natural gas from Afghanistan in that year, and from Iran in 1970, and was a net importer of natural gas from 1970 through 1973. To the Soviets, this made good business sense because the gas was cheap and ultimately they expected to export at least a portion of it. Some observers have viewed this, however, as an indication that a shortage of energy exists in the Soviet Union. In fact, the Soviet Union was only awaiting the opening of supply and export pipelines. Once some of these pipelines were completed in 1973 and 1974, Soviet natural gas also began to flow to the two Germanies, Italy, Belgium, Finland, and in 1975 to France. In 1974, the Soviet Union again became a net exporter, and it will probably remain such for many years. It has signed contracts for the export of about 25 to 30 billion cubic meters of gas to Western Europe. While some of this will be offset by increased imports of gas from Afghanistan and Iran, most of it will come from Soviet gas fields. In view of the fact that the Soviet Union is estimated to have five out of the ten largest gas fields in the world, there is little reason to doubt that the Soviet Union has the capacity to fulfil these commitments.

Political and Military Significance

We are now in a position to consider the political impact of Soviet oil and gas capabilities on the West. Even if the above estimates of Soviet export potential are overstated, the fact remains the Soviet Union is presently the only large industrialized country that is self-sufficient in petroleum and natural gas. Only Canada and Norway in the West are comparably self-sufficient. Ultimately, the Soviet Union may discover—like the United States—that its supplies of petroleum and gas are inadequate. But, because of its untapped reserves, this will be long after most of the rest of the industrialized world has done so. In time, its income-earning power may diminish, and its control over Eastern Europe may weaken if the East Europeans find themselves unable to obtain adequate supplies of energy. But the Soviet Union is less prone to international energy blackmail, and is in a better position to do its own blackmailing, than virtually all of the OECD countries.

Not only does the Soviet Union have adequate fuel reserves; it also has the ability to supply both its economic and military customers with energy dispatched via pipelines within the Soviet Union. The only above-ground exposure is in the Far East, which for the time being is supplied by train. But there are large fuel deposits in the area, and gradually the pipeline network is almost certain to be extended to link up these deposits with the end-users.

While this network of pipelines is a military asset for the Soviet

Union, it could easily become a source of weakness for Western Europe. Soviet pipelines supply not only Eastern Europe with gas and oil, but also Western Europe. If the provocation were great enough, presumably the pipelines could be turned off. At present, this would not leave any West European country completely without energy, but it would hurt. In particular, the gas importers, especially those like Austria which are almost wholly dependent upon the Soviet Union for gas, would suffer badly. In any case, the Soviet Union could use the threat of such a cut-off as a subtle weapon.

Thus, the Western allies and NATO find themselves in a much more exposed position. The bulk of the petroleum and natural gas reserves in the West are within the boundaries of the United States and Canada. This leaves Western Europe and Japan in a highly exposed position. Even the United States has now come to depend on others for supplemental fuel imports, and eventually Canada will, too. Inevitably, some of these supplies must be shipped in tankers, which are vulnerable to military attack. Japan and Western Europe are almost wholly dependent on ocean shipping for their liquid fuels. Even more than an oil embargo at the wellhead, an embargo on tankers or a naval blockade could be disastrous for the NATO countries. A hostile Soviet naval force could cause enormous harm—both economic and military.

It is clear that the Soviets are less exposed in this respect than we in the West. At the same time, they are in a position to be more disruptive than we. The big question is whether they would ever choose to be disruptive, and if so, what issues would cause them to take such a step.

If there were to be an all-out war, there is little doubt that the Soviet Union would not hesitate to use all the economic weapons at its disposal. That includes not only holding back on Soviet oil and gas deliveries, but also an attempt by the Soviet armed forces to disrupt the flow of non-Soviet tankers and petroleum supplies. Short of war, an individual country might find its oil supplies cut off when the Soviet Union feels its political aims have been thwarted. China, Yugoslavia, and Israel have been subjected to this type of economic blackmail in the past. In contrast, more recent Soviet behavior during the 1973 Yom Kippur War indicates that Moscow is quite capable of ignoring principles and continuing business as usual. Based on the record, in short, it is clear that the Soviet Union is capable of a wide variety of possible responses—from hostility to cooperation. The challenge is to predict what options the Soviets will choose, and when.

It is risky to establish any guidelines for prediction, however, because the Soviets have not behaved in a predictable fashion in the past. Their more recent behavior seems closely linked to the size of the economic reward to be earned. As the price of petroleum and the Soviet trade deficit have soared, Soviet political interests have been subordinated to more pragmatic concerns. Naturally, the higher the price of petroleum, the stronger the case for profits. This is not to say, however, that the Soviet Union will always opt for profit over politics.

Had Soviet troops been directly involved in the Yom Kippur War, perhaps profit would not have prevailed. Soviet actions during that conflict do illustrate one point. The more sources there are from which to buy petroleum, the harder it is to insure the uniform application of an embargo, and the more likely it is that one supplier will choose to take advantage of the others. Hence, it would be in the interest of the United States for the Soviet Union to compete in the world petroleum market, at least as long as it is not in a position to dominate or control other producers. In any event, there is little we can do to keep Soviet suppliers off the market. Even if we could, there seems to be little point in doing so. What is a paradox, however, is that while we seem to be contemplating steps which could well reduce our overall competitiveness in world petroleum markets, the Soviet Union is doing exactly the opposite—and, indeed, is vigorously improving its economic position by building up its own integrated international petroleum corporations.

6

Foreign Oil and National Security

KLAUS KNORR

Most Americans are agreed upon the need for an energy policy that will assure an adequate supply of energy at reasonable prices over the longer run. But there is as yet no strong consensus when it comes to particulars, that is, making the objectives specific and choosing the means by which they can be achieved. People tend to disagree on what constitutes an adequate supply, on what is a "reasonable" price to consumers, on the combination of measures that can be confidently expected to secure these results, and on how much must be sacrificed in the present in order to formulate a solution that will work in the future.

The focus of the present chapter is on one component of this policy problem, namely, the vulnerability of the United States caused by its dependence on foreign supplies of oil, and especially on oil imports from the OPEC countries—and among these, from the Arab members of the oil cartel. It is our thesis that this dependence constitutes a serious risk to the assured availability of energy in the United States; that this vulnerability can be exploited for politically coercive as well as economic purposes, and thus represents a political as well as economic weakness; and that any sensible US energy policy must include provisions for reducing this national vulnerability to acceptable proportions compatible with the economic, political, and military integrity of this country. In addition, the United States cannot be indifferent to the even greater vulnerability of its allies and main trading partners, particularly the West European nations and Japan. Any serious disruption of their economies threatens vital foreign policy interests of this country.

In the following, we will first analyze the nature of American vulnerability and then discuss ways and means for minimizing it.

The Arab Oil Embargo of 1973[1]

Prior to 1970, the international oil market was a buyer's market. It was firmly in the hands of the large international oil companies, mostly American. OPEC, though in existence since 1968, exercised little control. Prices were low because marginal production costs in the Middle East were low; and the world's industrial countries were rapidly increasing their imports partly because their economies and national income were growing vigorously, and partly because they were switching energy inputs away from other, less attractive fossil fuels to cheap oil. This situation began to be transformed rapidly and drastically in 1970. The buyer's market changed suddenly to a seller's market. The oil-producing countries began to sense the advent of monopolist power. At the same time, seeing that Western military and political power in the Middle East was effectively balanced by Soviet power, the Arab governments gained confidence in their ability to pursue independent nationalist policies and throw off all remnants of imperial influence and control. Within a few years, the Western oil companies were compelled to offer much higher prices for oil. Nevertheless, the oil imports of the industrial states continued to expand. From 1967 to 1973, those of Western Europe and Japan— taken together—nearly doubled, and those of the United States rose by more than 150 percent. By 1973, oil imports represented 63, 85, and 17 percent of the total energy supplies of Western Europe, Japan, and the United States, respectively. The United States alone required oil imports of approximately six million barrels a day.

Following the outbreak of the Yom Kippur War in October 1973 between Israel, on the one hand, and Egypt and Syria, OAPEC— that is, the Arab members of OPEC—cut oil production by 25

---

1 For a more detailed discussion of the Arab oil embargo, see Klaus Knorr, "The Limits of Economic and Mlitary Power," *Daedalus*, vol. 104 (1975), pp. 229-243; Hanns Maull, "Oil and Influence, The Oil Weapon Examined," Adelphi Papers No. 117 (London: International Institute for Strategic Studies, 1975).

percent, and placed an embargo on oil exports to the United States. The announced purpose was to compel the industrial importing nations, and in particular the United States, to modify their policies toward the Arab-Israeli conflict in favor of the Arab cause, and to induce Israel to return all Arab territories it had conquered in the earlier 1967 war and kept under occupation since then. This action on the part of the Arab countries was not merely the use of monopoly power for extracting monopoly profits—although that happened, too, as oil prices quadrupled to around $11 per barrel—but also the coercive employment of economic leverage in matters of high diplomacy.

The results were startling. Despite previous Arab warnings, the governments of the major oil-importing countries were caught by surprise, and some of them panicked. The West European countries and Japan quickly complied with Arab demands and issued official declarations in support of UN Security Council Resolution 242, which called on Israel to withdraw from Arab areas held since 1967. Two days after OAPEC decided to initiate the cutbacks in oil production, President Nixon asked Congress to approve $2.2 billion in military aid for Israel. The United States was decidedly less dependent on Arab oil than the other industrial countries. It could be inconvenienced by the embargo, and was; but it could manage if it had to. Washington protested the Arab action, and even issued vague warnings about a military riposte in the event that the Arab states proceeded to impose a "strangulating" embargo. More importantly, the United States set out promptly to negotiate a ceasefire between Israel and its Arab enemies. Washington clearly had independent reasons for sending Secretary Kissinger on his extraordinary venture in "shuttle" diplomacy. So long as the war in the Middle East continued, or threatened to erupt again after a ceasefire was arranged, there was always the risk of a dangerous confrontation with the Soviet Union. The United States, after all, was committed to protect the integrity of an Israeli state, while the Soviets backed the demands of the more radical Arab countries. At the same time, Washington was eager to maintain its influence in the region, especially *vis-à-vis* Moscow.

It can be argued that the Arabs' use of the oil weapon was only a limited success. Indeed, the embargo was lifted before all Arab demands had been met. But this was in part because the majority of OAPEC did not choose to impose a tougher and more prolonged interruption of oil supplies. Moreover, the industrial importing countries had been brought to recognize their extreme vulnerability, and this recognition alone would presumably persuade them not to cross important Arab interests in the future. To that extent, oil power will be effective in the future even though it is not brought into play, or is brought into play only by verbal reminders of what happened in 1973. At the same time, sharply higher oil prices fed inflation in the capitalist societies, reduced real income, and confronted them with potential pressure on their international balance of payments. The Arab countries, on the other hand, had tasted the fruits of power, which were especially sweet after more than a century of domination by the West; and the avalanche of hard currencies gave them the means to develop themselves economically, to invest abroad, to play an inflated role at international economic conferences, and to arm themselves with modern weaponry. At the same time, the OPEC countries emerged as the leaders of the Third World and its challenge to the international economic order that had been established under the auspices of the United States after World War II. In terms of international economic power and international political influence, the world had undergone an abrupt and substantial shift.

The Nature of Economic Power

In order to grasp clearly the possible consequences of the new economic leverage in the hands of the main oil-exporting countries, it is important that we understand the nature of international economic power. Only when we have clarified the concept of economic power can we hope to speculate with some confidence on its future use and effectiveness.

An actor A possesses economic leverage over B if B is more dependent on what he needs from A than A is dependent on what he needs from B. This is a relationship of asymmetrical interdependence long familiar to students of economic monopoly. Monopoly power is the greater, the more completely the monopolist controls the supply of something of value, and the more urgent or inelastic is the market demand for the valued thing. Monopoly power can be employed for various purposes, two of which are of major interest to us here. The classically familiar use is to charge monopoly prices for monopoly profit. OPEC has done this by sharply raising the price of oil. Monopoly power can also be used for purposes of coercion, that is, for attempting to change the behavior of another actor. The monopolist can attempt to do so by threatening to withhold deliveries from the supply under his control, and by actually cutting supplies in the event that the other actor fails to yield to the threat. OAPEC did so in the case of the oil embargo of 1973.

Now, the monopolist will not attempt such coercion unless he is willing to accept the costs of doing so. The costs are manifold. Withholding supplies will reduce revenues, and quite possibly employment. Other costs may involve countermeasures by the threatened actor, who may be able to withhold the supply of things under his control, and who may resort to noneconomic countermeasures— for example, of a military kind if relative military strength permits this. As long as the actor possessing economic leverage proceeds rationally, he will bring his power into coercive play only if he expects the gains to exceed the costs. He might underestimate these costs, which could affect the outcome; but he would act on the basis of his estimate. While the success of the attempt at coercion depends in the first place on how dependent the threatened party is on access to the monopolist's supply, it also depends on the costs of complying with the monopolist's demand. These costs have two components: first, of course, the value of the behavior that the target actor is asked to change; and second, the psychological costs of having been compelled to comply. The target actor will be coerced only if he expects the costs of having to do without the withheld supply exceed the costs of compliance.

We can now apply this conceptual framework to the events of 1973 in order to get a sharper evaluation of the economic leverage available to OPEC and OAPEC; and then speculate about its future use against the United States and other industrial nations.

The Bases of OPEC and OAPEC Power

The OPEC countries control so large a proportion of total oil exports that the importing states cannot satisfy their needs by going elsewhere. Moreover, oil-exporting countries that are not members of OPEC (including the Soviet Union, China, and Canada) naturally charge OPEC prices except for special arrangements. (The Soviet Union charges less than OPEC prices for oil exported to its East European Communist allies.) At the same time, oil imports are so vital to the importing countries—to their very economic and social life—and available substitute sources of energy so inadequate that their need for OPEC oil is extremely urgent. Demand is not completely inelastic to price; but it is—over the shorter term, at least—highly inelastic. As long as OPEC remains unified, thus preserving its monopoly power, it is therefore in a position to dictate prices. This does not mean that there is no upward limit to the price level that OPEC may want to fix. There are costs to the monopolist even when his objective is only monopolist profit. Over the longer run, he will be concerned about the effect of very high prices in stimulating the production of energy from other sources. But even over the shorter run, he is not interested in killing the goose that lays the golden eggs. A level of prices that would seriously disrupt the economic life of the industrial importing countries is not in the interest of the OPEC states as a group, nor is it in their interest to impose additional burdens on the world's underdeveloped and poor societies that also depend on imports of oil. The rational monopolist will push prices to the level where he expects to maximize his revenue over the longer run.

Regarding the use of the oil embargo for extracting political gains, OAPEC's control over oil exports was evidently sufficient *vis-à-vis* Japan and Western Europe, but much less so *vis-à-vis* the United States, which was the principal target of this attempt at coercion. With substantial domestic oil production of its own, a great deal of oil in transit on the seas, imports from other oil-exporting countries, and the ability of the oil companies to adapt the pattern of shipments to minimize the impact of the embargo, this country could be inconvenienced but was not very vulnerable. By means of rationing and curtailing wasteful uses of energy, the United States could have managed if the embargo had been more rigorous and prolonged, but not without serious economic dislocations. In sum, Arab economic leverage on this country was not as effective as it was with Western Europe and Japan, but it was sufficiently disruptive to provide a clear economic and political warning.

On the other hand, the Arab use of this leverage was subject to appreciable restraints. To be sure, economic costs were negligible because the simultaneous rise in oil prices kept revenues up even when export volumes were cut. The important restraints were political. Saudi Arabia had been enjoying fairly friendly relations with the

United States. Most of the Arab countries were not interested in antagonizing this country because they were aware that the reach of American military power in the Middle East balanced Soviet power, and that this balance was essential to the freedom of action of the countries in the area. Nor could the OAPEC governments be sure, in the event of a severe and protracted embargo, that the United States would not be tempted to counter economic aggression by resort to military threats. These considerations go far toward explaining why the embargo was mild, and was lifted before all Arab demands had been met. Finally, the political costs of compliance were not high for Western Europe and Japan. No doubt, both leaders and publics were conscious of being subject to coercive pressure, and were not insensitive to the ignominy involved in submission. But all they were asked to do was to declare their support for UN Security Council Resolution 242, a position which the West Europeans had been approaching previously in any event. On other grounds, the United States was also interested in a settlement of the Arab-Israeli conflict on terms acceptable to both sides. Yet as a great power, the United States would have been loath to yield to economic pressure in matters of high policy. To submit to it would have been sensed as too demeaning. In the event, the United States did not have to face the issue in these terms. Washington remained essentially uncoerced at the time; but it received a disturbing message with reference to the future that would be dangerous to ignore.

Future Uses of the Oil Weapon

The newly wealthy oil-exporting states will obviously enjoy vastly more influence on international economic issues than they had before 1973; and there is every indication that they will apply this influence not only on behalf of their own interests, but also for Third World demands for a new economic order. It is also clear that the oil-exporting countries can and will use their wealth to support friendly states (as some of them are now giving financial support to Egypt and Syria), and to buy political support from poorer countries (as OAPEC countries have done when acquiring the support of sub-Saharan African states in the United Nations for the Arab cause against Israel). But what interests us here primarily is the renewed use of the oil weapon against the West for purposes of coercion in matters of high policy.

Arab spokesmen have repeatedly stated that another embargo on oil exports might have to be considered if the prospects for a settlement of the Arab-Israeli conflict remain elusive. The industrial oil-importing countries are not insensitive to the pressure implied in this unspecific threat. Certainly the West European governments have singly and collectively gone. out of their way to court Arab goodwill. The results have been far from reassuring. Attempts made by individual countries in 1974 and 1975 to secure special deals with OPEC countries by offering diplomatic and economic concessions proved abortive. The Arab governments in particular had the upper hand in this sort of bargaining, and accepted concessions without giving meaningful assurances in return.[2] More recently, the nine members of the European Community began what is meant to be a series of dialogues with a team representing the Arab states. Again, the Arabs were bargaining from a position of strength. They showed little interest in proposed guidelines for stimulating exports to and investment in Arab lands. These were things that petrodollars could buy in any case. Instead they kept insisting that the Europeans do more to put pressure on Israel.[3] The threat of the oil weapon achieves considerable results in this way, for it evidently reduces the freedom of action of the West European nations, and also of Japan, and makes them continuously apprehensive. The evidence is much more ambiguous in the case of the United States. But it is reasonable to assume that the possibility of another oil embargo is a weighty factor in this country's policy toward the Middle East. To an undefinable extent, it restricts American freedom of action.

But is the vague OAPEC threat more than a bluff? How probable is it that the oil weapon will be brought into play in the future? Nobody can be sure. But by applying our analytical framework and the knowledge we gained in 1973, we are able to narrow down the possibilities.

The first question is whether OAPEC's degree of monopoly power has appreciably changed since 1973. This power rests, to begin with, on OAPEC cohesion, that is, on the ability of these countries to act in unison. The behavior of its members at OPEC meetings on the matter of oil prices indicates no essential change in this respect.

---

2 See Curt Gasteyger, Louis Camu, and Jack N. Behrman, eds., *Energy, Inflation and International Economic Relations*, Atlantic Institute Studies II (New York: Praeger, 1975), pp. 58-73.

3 "Sandblasted: Euro-Arab Dialogue," *Economist* (London), May 29, 1976, p. 67.

While the economic interests of OAPEC members in this matter are not identical, these differences have not been permitted so far to erode essential agreement on the value of maintaining monopoly power. It would be surprising if it were otherwise. Unsheathing the oil weapon in earnest requires agreement among the OAPEC countries. The only conceivable political purpose for wielding the oil weapon at the present time is the Arab desire to bring about a satisfactory settlement with Israel. While these countries are not in full agreement on the precise nature of this settlement, or on a strategy for achieving it, their basic agreement is in all likelihood strong enough to render the imposition of another oil embargo feasible in the event of another Arab war with Israel. While such action is less probable, in the absence of such a war, for terminating the present stalemate and setting significant negotiations once more in motion, it cannot be ruled out that an Arab coalition could be organized with sufficient control over oil exports to make this feasible. As long as Saudi Arabia, the Persian Gulf states, Libya, and Algeria participate, the span of control is sufficient for launching a coercive policy. Saudi Arabia holds the key position; without it, coalition control over oil supplies would be inadequate.

Not a great deal has changed since 1973 with respect to the vital dependence of the industrial nations on oil imports. Japan, and especially the West European countries, are at present somewhat less vulnerable than three years ago. Their governments will not panic in the event of another embargo, as they did in 1973. They have appreciably augmented their reserve stocks and prepared themselves for emergency rationing. They have also kept their energy consumption from increasing at previous rates. The recent business recession has helped in this respect, and sharply higher fuel prices have caused consumers to economize.

For reasons discussed below, the United States has done markedly less to build up stocks and reduce wasteful and inefficient uses of energy. The previous growth of annual energy consumption was halted for a time, in large part as a result of the business recession. But more recently, as domestic oil output has been contracting, imports have been rising. By now, the United States imports more than seven million barrels a day, 80 percent of which (amounting to over 40 percent of total consumption) comes from OPEC exporters. At present, however, the United States should still be able to cope with an OAPEC embargo, even a prolonged one, provided it musters the will to refuse coercion by this means. This latter condition is crucial, because a complete and protracted embargo would deeply disrupt the economy and inflict widespread and severe deprivations on the mass of consumers. The temptation to seek relief by yielding to Arab demands would be strong.

Even if we conclude that OAPEC can mobilize roughly as much monopoly power over oil supplies as it did in 1973, and that the vulnerability of the industrial importing states has not changed much so far, Arab decisionmakers would still have to take into account the costs and risks of wielding the oil weapon; and they would also have to consider the level of demands—the costs of compliance to the importing countries—at which effective coercion would be likely.

The considerations that would serve to restrain the Arab governments are fundamentally the same as before. Some of these governments would dislike losing export revenues while non-Arab exporting countries were maintaining, and probably increasing, theirs. They are not interested in causing severe economic disorder in the economies of the oil-importing countries, even though the threat to inflict such a critical degree of damage would increase their coercive power. Moreover, most of them are not interested in weakening the United States as an international balancing power, or in inducing this country to consider military reprisals.

Regarding the level of political demands that OAPEC governments could make (that is the price for lifting the embargo), the fact is that although the West European nations and Japan could be compelled to express declarations of sympathy for the Arab cause, to put pressure on the United States, and perhaps even to sever diplomatic or commercial relations with Israel, these countries have little influence to bring to bear on Israeli policy. The country that has such influence is, of course, the United States, which would therefore be the ultimate target of any economic power play by the Arabs. Arab leaders know by now, however, that American influence on the Israelis, which arises from the latter's dependence on US arms and other support, is not without limits, especially because the strength of genuine American identification with the security of Israel makes it impossible for Washington to abandon Israel, or even threaten to do so. These facts set limits to the costs of compliance that the United States would be able to absorb even if the economic inconveniences and dislocations of an oil embargo were to tempt it to make some concessions to Arab demands.

This set of interlocking constraints impinging on both sides would seem to circumscribe rather narrowly the freedom of action of the major actors, so long as they continue to evaluate and exercise their choices rationally. The degree to which rationality will prevail is not predictable. But the chances are that deviations from it would not be extreme; and that, if the OAPEC states were to initiate another round of open economic warfare by embargoing oil exports, they might well be satisfied with doing so to an extent that would hurt but would not seriously threaten the viability of the oil-importing countries. The prudent purpose would be to add one bargaining counter to others that the Arabs could invest in exploiting a new international crisis over their conflict with Israel.

The Future Problem

So far, we have described the factors that would operate now or in the immediate future if the Arab governments decided to unleash the oil weapon again. We have been careful not to exaggerate the resulting pressures on the United States, and concluded that this country could manage if it chose to defy an Arab attempt at coercion with respect to American policy in Israel. But even now, defiance would be costly because the United States depends on imports for about 40 percent of its oil supply. A shortfall of even ten or 15 percent would require prompt and rigorous rationing, and entail substantial dislocations of the economy and of employment.[4] It would not be easy to stand firm, especially if an extension of the oil embargo to Western Europe and Japan, and the infliction of acute economic distress and upheaval on these countries, would be part of the cost of American defiance.

The future looks more bleak. The American position would be much weaker, and American choices more desperate, if we project current trends ahead and contemplate the consequences of an OAPEC embargo not now but four or five or six years hence. It is possible, of course, that a settlement of the Arab-Israeli conflict will remove the danger altogether. But it would perhaps be too sanguine, in the

---

4 The 1973 embargo caused United States oil imports to fall only from 6.6 million barrels per day in November 1973 to 5.1 millions in January 1974. Thereafter, imports rose to 5.5 million. But the cut of less than 14 percent proved disruptive enough.

light of past history, to count on such a fortunate turn of events. Yet if the United States fails to reverse its present energy policy, its vulnerability to the oil weapon is bound to grow each year. The Federal Energy Authority estimates that the country will import 45 percent of its oil supply in 1977; and this proportion is likely to rise to around 50 percent by 1980. This is likely to happen because the resumption of economic growth and an increase of employment in this country will inevitably augment the demand for energy, while any expansion of domestic oil and gas production cannot be expected under present conditions of federal price control. The resumption of economic growth in Western Europe and Japan will also raise the demand for foreign oil in these countries, except for Britain and Norway where offshore production in the North Sea will increasingly come on stream. In other words, if present policies persist, the United States will permit itself to become steadily more vulnerable to an Arab oil embargo. It is in effect strengthening the economic leverage enjoyed by the OAPEC states, which need do nothing but watch— probably with amazement. And if the Arab governments decide to exploit this leverage some years from now, the United States will face an appalling crisis. The costs of defiance will then be extremely high. Washington's freedom of action will be constricted to a point that is surely incompatible with its role as a great international power and with the international responsibilities it has assumed.

Despite occasional speculation to the contrary, it is an illusion to believe that the United States could rescue itself by recourse to military power. This is not a feasible, let alone sensible, option for countering the oil weapon and preserving American freedom of action. No doubt, this country has the capabilities to inflict enormous damage on the Arab oil-exporting countries. But any threat to do so would have very little credibility, because its execution would be seen by everyone to do more harm than good to the United States itself. Not only would the Arabs fight back. They would also destroy oil production and transportation facilities; and they could count on Soviet support and on intense anti-American reactions throughout the rest of the world, most likely including Western Europe and Japan. A further radicalization of Arab politics would be inevitable, and the United States would end up by earning the enmity of those Arab countries with which it now has basically good relations. To top it all, the disruption in oil exports would continue.

We have concentrated on the possible re-employment of the oil weapon because this is by far the most likely problem to which the dependence of the industrial countries on foreign oil may give rise, so long as the Arab conflict with Israel continues to smolder. Further rises by OPEC in the real price of oil are, of course, more likely; and their consequences in terms of income losses and inflationary pressures in the importing countries are obviously undesirable. But they are far less serious than the imposition of an oil embargo. Indeed, higher oil prices would stimulate less wasteful and more efficient use of energy in the importing states, and encourage the production of energy from alternative sources. These are all things that the countries would be wise to foster in order to reduce their vulnerability to oil embargoes. Conversely, doing these things in order to curtail this vulnerability would also diminish over time the ability of OPEC to raise prices.

The only other danger that has received some attention is the vulnerability of oil shipments from the Persian Gulf to hostile military interference. The problem might be a local war in the area, whether a civil war or one between neighboring states. Such events could well occur, and would present Washington with difficult problems of foreign policy, especially if the Soviet Union intervened. They would also reduce oil production and shipments for a time. But only a part of the producing area would be affected; and the burden of adjustment, though considerable, should therefore be manageable even if Saudi Arabia were involved. And again, any action by the United States and other oil-importing countries designed to minimize their vulnerability to the oil weapon would clearly also minimize the burden of adjustment.

The remaining danger sometimes mentioned is the interruption of oil shipments by hostile naval forces that might mine narrow passages and perhaps attack tankers as well. This danger seems remote at the present time. Any such hostile action by a local naval power would have only local effect, and would presumably lead to counteraction under international auspices and with a high claim to international legitimacy. The situation would be less tractable if the Soviet Union decided to support the local power or powers, and if exit from the Persian Gulf were completely blocked. Yet this is probably a farfetched scenario. The oil-exporting countries, after all, have a strong interest, regardless of their political complexion, in selling oil. Moreover, other producing countries might well be ready to increase their exports, and a temporary cut of overall supplies should be bearable if the industrial importing states act with coordination and dispatch.

The only power with sufficient capabilities to act on a larger scale in cutting lines of maritime transportation is the Soviet Union. But it is hard to imagine such a contingency short of an outbreak of general war. Any joint military action by the Soviet Union and the Middle East oil exporters to cut oil exports is hard to imagine, because if oil shipments are to be denied to the West, all that is necessary is to refuse to load the tankers and to shut down production. It is just as hard to imagine that the Soviet Union would see it to its advantage to cut oil shipments by military means against the wish of the Middle Eastern countries, and at the same time accepting the risk of a naval war with the United States—a war that would have a high potential for escalating to all-out conflict. In sum, the serious contingency regarding Middle Eastern oil which the United States should be primarily concerned with is the threat of an oil embargo.

What Energy Policy for the United States?

The preceding analysis seems to establish a strong case for a US policy that protects American freedom of action internationally as well as the American economy and consumer, and is in keeping with its status and responsibilities as a great power and as an ally of the other industrial oil-importing countries. The United States may not do so, and political paralysis may prevent it from doing so. But this should not be allowed to happen except in full public recognition of the formidable risks involved. Energy is crucial to all basic functions of industrial society, and to its comforts as well. This is why the oil weapon is potentially so dangerous. No other weapon is in the same class. There is no certainty, to be sure, that another oil embargo will occur. But an appreciable possibility is enough to justify countermeasures when the looming consequences of an embargo are so grave. Furthermore, taking out insurance against this contingency will have a deterrent effect, and make it less likely—indeed unlikely—that the threat will be made real.

The first shock of OAPEC's oil embargo led President Nixon in 1974 to launch "Project Independence," aimed in principle at making the United States independent of unreliable oil supplies within ten years; and President Ford proposed a similar program to the Congress in January 1975. The purpose of these initiatives seems to us to be eminently sound; and the purpose can be satisfied if the nation can mobilize the political will to accept the means.

The United States does not require strict energy independence or total energy dependability. A more modest goal will suffice. The United States can afford to import "unreliable" oil up to an amount that it can do without in an emergency. More precisely, the acceptable margin of "unreliable" oil is one that, if cut off even for a protracted period of time, causes some discomfort (for example, some degree of gasoline rationing) but leaves all functions essential to economic and political viability fully intact. The principal policies by which the goal of reasonable energy dependability can be achieved are clear. They fall into three classes.

— First, the accumulation of substantial reserve stocks of oil, and the preparation of an emergency scheme for rationing consumption that has been approved by Congress and can be put into operation without delay.
— Second, the stimulation of domestic production of oil and gas, and of some gradual shift to nonoil sources of energy, especially coal, both for the production of electricity and, over the longer run, of synthetic fuels.
— Third, the enforcement of energy conservation, that is, of less wasteful and more efficient uses of energy.

The detailed structuring of such a program is inevitably controversial. This is so for three main reasons. First, the effectiveness— especially the cost-effectiveness of any particular measure—is a matter of guesswork even among experts. For example, we still know little about the price-elasticity of energy demand in various uses over the longer run; we can only guess about the capital costs of producing gasoline from coal; we do not know the size of oil deposits off the Atlantic Coast, or the costs of their exploitation; and so forth.

Second, consumers and citizens alike will naturally be sensitive to the costs to them of any part of the program, especially to higher prices of gasoline, fuel oil, and electricity. But security is worth some price, and higher energy costs will have to be accepted even if the country relies increasingly on more expensive OPEC oil. How these costs are distributed among the public is, of course, fundamentally a political decision. But it should be possible to design a reasonably fair system that is acceptable to a majority of the people. For example, if higher fuel prices are the best way to diminish marginally wasteful uses of energy, lower-income groups can be compensated by modifications of the income tax. Or, if higher prices to domestic producers are needed to encourage oil and gas production, excess profit taxes can be used to prevent more than a reasonable return on corporate capital.

Third, any increase in the domestic production of fuel will have undesirable side-effects, particularly in terms of environmental deterioration. These "externalities" should obviously be taken into account in the overall design of a US energy program, but they should not be allowed to stand rigidly in the way of achieving other social values such as a dependable energy supply. The problem is one of trade-offs among various values and costs at the margin. For example, some environmental deterioration resulting from expanded coal production may well be acceptable as a price for achieving a more reliable supply of energy, especially if other components of the program (such as the discouragement of wasteful uses of energy) reduce environmental pollution at the same time.

One side issue that threatens to interfere with the establishment of a viable energy policy for the United States involves critical Congressional attitudes toward the big oil companies. A consequence of this disposition has been to limit prices that can be charged for domestic oil and gas, with the effect that, while consumers benefit in the short run, domestic output and investment in new exploration and production are discouraged. The other consequence is the current endeavor to subject the big oil companies to divestiture. The motivations behind this move are unclear but evidently mixed. One springs from the hope that the enforcement of more competition within the industry will serve to lower fuel prices. As many experts have pointed out, the oil industry is more competitive than most large American industries, and divestiture is highly unlikely to affect the price of oil products.

Another Congressional motivation is apparently the feeling that the oil companies, even if not responsible for the dramatic events that have revolutionized the world oil market, are out to derive excessive profits from this change. It can be taken for granted that these corporations, like all private enterprise, are out to make as much money as they can; and it is perfectly sound public policy to see to it that the achievement of this private objective coincides with the public interest. Clearly, the nation needs an assured supply of energy, and the satisfaction of this need requires large new investments by the oil companies (and other enterprises producing energy). For these to be forthcoming, the companies need access to capital and a profit incentive. The proper public instrument for providing these requisites while denying excess profits is an appropriate structure of corporate taxation. It is hard to see how the dismemberment of the industry will result in a strong incentive for exploration and production, and greater access to capital.

Finally, much of the Congressional support for divestiture seems to issue from a populist mood that is suspicious of, and hostile to, all concentrations of corporate power, including the oil companies. That issue goes to the heart of this country's economic system, and should be debated in general and rational terms, and not acted upon opportunistically with reference to a particular industry. Moreover, the oil industry—the target of opportunity at the moment—is extravagantly ill-chosen. The proper entrepreneurial functioning of this vital branch of national production has never been as much in the national interest as at the present time. To subject the oil industry to all the problems and tribulations of dismemberment now would mean that management resources would be diverted for a number of years from the vital tasks that must be performed if the United States is to minimize its dangerous and disturbing dependence on Middle Eastern oil. Nor could divestiture of the big oil companies fail to weaken the United States in dealing with the OPEC governments.[5] The divestiture proposal is, on every count, extremely inopportune.

The key problem for the Congress is surely its reluctance to legislate measures that will raise energy costs to voters. The temptation is to discount the risk of another OAPEC embargo (which, after all, may not happen again), and to oppose actions that increase the price of energy even if doing so magnifies American vulnerability to the outside world. It is a temptation that should be resisted in the national interest.

The contrary and divisive conceptions of the American energy problem—especially as between the Administration and the Congress—that have made it impossible for the United States to formulate a viable

---

5 For a detailed exploration of this problem, see Department of State News Release on "International Problems Foreseen in Breaking Up Oil Companies," June 3, 1976.

energy policy must be overcome by a new readiness on all sides to build the public consensus upon which such a policy must rest. And above all, the policy must include safeguards against external vulnerability. The paralysis of the past two years is a luxury that this country can no longer afford.

7

Energy and National Security

WILLIAM J. CASEY

The energy crisis presents challenges of historic dimensions to American security and welfare, as well as to world society. It has given other nations unacceptable leverage over our national security and foreign policy. It has already tilted the world's wealth and savings sharply toward the oil-exporting nations; it has caused simultaneous unemployment and inflation in the United States and around the world; and it has put most of the oil-consuming nations dangerously in debt.

We have failed to respond effectively to this threat to our national security and economic welfare. Most of the components of our present national energy policy either have intensified or will intensify our energy predicament.

—We have talked about achieving energy independence in our own country, while all that is realistically attainable in the short run is a reduction and a broadening of our dependency so that no cartel can cut us off as sharply as the Arab states did in 1973.
—We have put the illusory short-term advantage of having American consumers and voters pay only half the price for fuel that prevails in Europe and Japan above our true long-term interest in reducing the use and increasing the supply of energy resources.

—We have watched the funds piled up by the oil-exporting nations
flow into loans to maintain oil consumption, instead of attracting
it into investments to conserve oil use and diversify energy
sources.

—Now, some of us are indulging in the fantasy that breaking up
the organizations which have the capability to find new oil and
bring it to market will contribute to overcoming our energy
shortage.

Since late 1973, when oil supplies became a much-discussed problem in the United States, the issue of prices and supplies has been
too often viewed as a domestic problem replete with American villains,
American victims, and American solutions. Adequate oil supply is
not an isolated American problem. It is a worldwide problem born
of decades of increasing world demand for a cheap and bountiful fuel,
and the consequent leverage gained and suddenly applied by producers
and exporters of that fuel.

While importing substantial and increasing amounts of oil, the
United States has become entangled in a web of international political,
economic, and military relationships. The authors of this collection
of essays have discussed the "oil problem" in the proper context not
only of domestic supplies and production, but also of a complicated
and sensitive international imbroglio. They have moved the focus of
discussion out of the United States and into the Middle East: the
situs of the oil, the money, the cartel, the leverage, the war, the strategic
interests of the United States and the Soviet Union.

With the two superpowers at a military stand-off in the Middle
East, the OPEC nations were able to bring off a remarkable financial
coup in quadrupling the price of oil in 1973.[1] This step added billions
to their reserves, which an early World Bank estimate (since revised
downward) put at $650 billion by 1980. Even so, Saudi Arabia com-
mands foreign currency reserves of $45 billion at present. And money
is power—power to buy the weapons needed to become a major military power, for one thing. Both Saudi Arabia and Iran have spent
lavishly on their military establishments. The presence of such massive
armaments in Arab hands adds to Egypt's capacity to exert pressure

---

1 The following three paragraphs are based on Janet Kelly, "International Monetary Relations and National Security," in Klaus Knorr and Frank N. Trager, eds., *Economic Issues and
National Security* (forthcoming).

on Israel. Even Venezuela casts a longer shadow in Latin America, as its monetary reserves pile up. Never has money spoken more loudly.

Nor is the effect limited to the martial arena. A number of OPEC countries have traditionally held their foreign currency reserves in sterling—a legacy of imperial days, in part, but also a policy dating back to the time when sterling was the world's reserve currency. When some of them, such as Abu Dhabi, decided not to keep all of their growing reserves in London, the resulting rumors triggered further erosion of the battered pound, which the British authorities were powerless to counteract. OPEC's monetary reserves have already enabled some countries to make sizeable investments in large Western companies, as Iran has done in purchasing 25 percent of Krupp. The Arab governments have denied any interest in taking over major Western companies, but the capability is there.

Another way in which OPEC reserves can be used is to influence rates of exchange. The massive movement of funds into, or out of, a currency can—as in the case of the British pound—result in sizable fluctuations. Theoretically, OPEC reserves could also be brought to bear against the dollar, though OPEC's interests would seem to be better served by the preservation of the value of the dollar. The United States conceives it to be in its interest to have OPEC reserves held in dollars, and for that reason (among many others) will presumably try to maintain the dollar. But clearly, the ownership of huge sums of dollars by foreign governments that might someday move into other currencies is a change in the balance of monetary power. The game is being played for very high stakes.

The authors emphasize that there are sensible approaches that the United States can take to protect itself economically and strategically, although the solutions will require time and considerable planning. They would be based upon the fact that the United States has substantial reserves of oil *and* gas *and* other nonoil energy resources, as well as the capacity to utilize existing resources more efficiently. Such substitutions for imported oil would make obvious economic and strategic sense. A shift into coal or uranium-based energy would improve the US terms of trade over the long run. A reasonable degree of self-sufficiency in energy would help to insulate the country from further economic sanctions, such as the Arab oil embargo of 1973-74.

We need to buy the time to develop our coal and nuclear options, and ultimately to shift to energy sources which are not exhaustible.

Only greater economy in the use of energy, increased supplies of oil and gas, and the intensified use of coal and nuclear power on a worldwide basis can restore a satisfactory economic and financial balance in the world economy during our lifetime. New energy supplies sufficient to give us security against military and foreign policy pressures, and against manipulation of our economy by capricious price increases in its basic energy needs, can only come:

—in the short run—five to ten years—from new findings of oil and gas;
—in the ten- to 20-year time-frame, from intensified use of nuclear and coal options; and
—in the long-term frame, breakthroughs yielding inexhaustible supplies—solar, breeder reactor, fusion.

A major US asset is its technology and experience in finding oil and gas. Over the 30 years since 1945, we have more than tripled production and quadrupled known reserves. Since the 1974 embargo, vast new reserves have been discovered in the North Sea, in Mexico, and in the Pacific and Aegean.

Instead of a thoughtful and determined pursuit of these multiple alternatives, we have lost over two years in an interminable energy debate in Congress. The international oil companies have been blamed entirely for the problem—for complicity, or for negligence. More than a hundred bills have emanated from 30 committees of the Congress during the last three years, each in piecemeal fashion attempting to solve the oil problem, but none representing a significant step toward energy self-sufficiency. In fact, some of these actions have been counterproductive.

For example, Congress has virtually removed the percentage depletion tax incentive from oil and gas, while retaining price controls on crude oil, natural gas, and gasoline. But the proposed solutions of perhaps greatest consequence presented during these three years involve oil company divestiture—both vertical and horizontal. Horizontal divestiture would prevent oil companies from remaining or becoming involved in other energy fields. Vertical divestiture, as set forth in S. 2387, has been proposed as a panacea for most of the nation's energy problems.

Proponents claim that this bill will increase competition, provide the lowest possible prices, and weaken and perhaps destroy the OPEC cartel. But it is difficult to find persuasive support for these claims. The authors of this book are in general agreement that S. 2387 is, if anything, a nonremedy. It is a solution to a problem that does not exist, and an improper solution to the one that does. Regardless of the structure of our domestic oil industry, free world oil exports will be controlled by OPEC. OPEC will continue to control the world oil price as long as its members can agree among themselves to do so. At the same time, the United States is vulnerable because of heavy and increasing dependence on oil imports from that cartel.

If the solution does not strike at the problem, it may very well create problems of its own. Peter Bator has outlined in detail the effects of ten or 20 years of litigation, confusion in the industry and capital markets, and diversion of managerial purpose. The loser would be the United States; OPEC would remain untouched. Vertical divestiture proponents would cripple the very markets and industries which must help us solve our energy problems. In short, some members of Congress naively believe they are "protecting" consumers under the assumption that consumers and industries are natural antagonists. The petroleum industry's record proves that assumption to be false. Under the proposed solutions of divestiture proponents, we would all lose.

Any successful energy policy will require the thoughtful, coordinated actions of government, business, and consumers. Any program will require decades of development. The development of coal, for example, illustrates the complexities which a national energy policy must confront. Both the President and the Congress have called for increased coal production in order to reduce the nation's dependence on foreign oil. Coal is an abundant resource, representing 90 percent of the nation's proven energy reserves. Now providing only 18 percent of the energy we consume, coal should be a natural, perhaps dominant, part of our mid-term energy program. But many of those who want to isolate the United States economy from Arab leverage are, at the same time, hampering the increased, orderly development of coal.

The American coal industry is fragmented, undercapitalized and not easily capable of rapid expansion. Production declined from 1948 through 1974, as the nation shifted to cheaper and more plentiful oil and gas. In 1948, coal sold in the United States for an average of $4.99 per ton; some 20 years later, the price was unchanged. Low prices, declining production, and consequent low profit margins stimulated little new investment, modernization, or resolution of long-standing labor problems. Yet the FEA has projected the need for an increase in coal production from 604 million tons in 1974 to 1,040 million tons in 1985—an annual growth rate of more than five percent.

That increase is dependent upon price trends, the demand for electricity (coal's primary market), the leasing and development of resources under federal lands, and federal and state environmental policies, particularly those regulating the emission of sulphur oxides. Once these problems are confronted, time lags will be inevitable. Development of a new mine requires six to eight years. The electric generating plant it will supply takes from five to eight years to construct. The industry will need substantial capital to meet projections of demand. The FEA estimates a ten-year requirement of around $20 billion, compared with current capitalization of $5 or $6 billion. Thus, the new capital represents a monumental addition to an industry which has changed little during the previous 20 years.

Needed changes will not occur overnight; and as Carl Bagge, President of the National Coal Association, has said, the coal industry cannot do the job alone. "It would certainly be the height of hypocrisy for any member of Congress to legislate the exclusion of oil companies from the coal business as a protection for interfuel competition, and then vote for coal mining and coal utilization curbs that would severely diminish the supply of coal to the virtuously competitive marketplace. But this, incredible as it may seem, is precisely what appears to be happening in Congress." And coal is but one essential element in the national energy policy which must be established. The other elements are at least as complex, and they, too, will require time.

The energy task that lies ahead is a very large one. It will take the best expertise, the best organization, the best technology, and the best ability to apply technology that we can muster. The oil companies have these qualities. They have a record of accomplishment in breaking new ground to meet national needs. We have seen oil companies make crude oil into synthetic rubber, and develop high octane aviation gas, to meet security needs in World War II. We have seen them produce fertilizers, insecticides, and a variety of petrochemicals from oil and gas. The petroleum industry is ideally suited—in both size and expertise—to aid in developing coal and other alternate energy sources. In fact, many of these energy sources, such as oil shale and coal gasification and liquefaction, depend partially on petroleum industry technology for their development.

It is axiomatic that a nation's well-being depends upon a strong defense and a healthy economy. Government and industry must work together to stimulate the development and more efficient use of all of our domestic energy resources, in order to counterbalance the unacceptable political and economic leverage of OPEC. The purpose of this collection of essays has been to clarify one important aspect of the current debate. We hope that it may help lead toward a sensible energy policy.

About the Authors

M. A. ADELMAN is Professor of Economics at the Massachusetts Institute of Technology, where he has taught since 1948. An authority on monopoly and competition, he has specialized on the energy and petroleum industries since 1960, and is the author of *The Supply and Price of Natural Gas* (1962), *Alaskan Oil* (1970), and *The World Petroleum Market* (1972), among other works.

WILLIAM J. CASEY has had a distinguished career in government and law, including service as Chairman of the Securities and Exchange Commission (1971-72), Under Secretary of State for Economic Affairs (1972-74), and Chairman of the Export-Import Bank (1974-76). He is now in private practice in Washington.

EDWARD W. ERICKSON, Professor of Economics and Business at North Carolina State University, is a leading authority on the petroleum industry. He has served on the National Petroleum Council (1975-76) and numerous other public-interest boards and panels. He is editor (with L. Waverman) of *The Energy Question, An International Failure of Policy* (1974), and has also written extensively in the field.

MARSHALL I. GOLDMAN is Associate Director of the Russian Research Center at Harvard University, and Chairman of the Department of Economics at Wellesley College, where he holds the Chair of the Class of 1919. His most recent book is *Detente and Dollars, Doing Business with the Soviets* (1975).

WILLIAM A. JOHNSON is Professor of Economics at George Washington University, and Director of its Energy Policy Research Project. He has served in the government with the President's Council of Economic Advisors, the Treasury Department, and the Federal Energy Office, and is the author of two books and numerous scholarly papers.

KLAUS KNORR is Professor of Public and International Affairs at the Woodrow Wilson School, Princeton University, and editor of the quarterly journal, *World Politics*. He is the author of numerous books and articles, including *Power and Wealth* (1973), *The Power of Nations* (1975), and *Historical Dimensions of Historical Security Problems* (1976).

RICHARD E. MESSICK is a Research Assistant with the George Washington University Energy Policy Research Project. A graduate of Indiana University, he has served as Legislative Assistant to US Senator William E. Brock, with responsibility for energy and natural resource issues.

FRANK N. TRAGER is Director of Studies at the National Strategy Information Center, and Professor of International Affairs and Director of the National Security Program at New York University. He has written and edited a shelf of books and articles on Asian Affairs and problems of national security.

* * *

Chapter Two of this volume, "Legal and Financial Consequences of Divestiture," reproduces the testimony of Peter A. Bator before the Subcommittee on Antitrust and Monopoly of the Senate Judiciary Committee, on January 27, 1976. Mr. Bator is a partner in the New York law firm of Davis Polk & Wardwell. He was graduated from Harvard Law School in 1954, where he also served as an editor of the *Harvard Law Review*. In addition to his present practice, he is a director of several companies and a member of numerous bar and other professional associations.

National Strategy Information Center, Inc.

STRATEGY PAPERS

Edited by Frank N. Trager and William Henderson
With the assistance of Dorothy E. Nicolosi

The Sino-Soviet Confrontation: Implications for the Future by Harold
C. Hinton, September 1976

Food, Foreign Policy, and Raw Materials Cartels by William
Schneider, February 1976

Strategic Weapons: An Introduction by Norman Polmar, October
1975

Soviet Sources of Military Doctrine and Strategy by William F. Scott,
July 1975

Detente: Promises and Pitfalls by Gerald L. Steibel, March 1975

Oil, Politics, and Sea Power: The Indian Ocean Vortex by Ian
W. A. C. Adie, December 1974

The Soviet Presence in Latin American by James D. Theberge,
June 1974

The Horn of Africa by J. Bowyer Bell, Jr., December 1973

*Research and Development and the Prospects for International Secur-
ity* by Frederick Seitz and Rodney W. Nichols, December 1973

Raw Material Supply in a Multipolar World by Yuan-li Wu, October
1973

The People's Liberation Army: Communist China's Armed Forces
by Angus M. Fraser, August 1973 (Out of print)

Nuclear Weapons and the Atlantic Alliance by Wynfred Joshua, May
1973

How to Think About Arms Control and Disarmament by James E.
Dougherty, May 1973

The Military Indoctrination of Soviet Youth by Leon Goure, January
1973 (Out of print)

The Asian Alliance: Japan and United States Policy by Franz Michael and Gaston J. Sigur, October 1972

Iran, The Arabian Peninsula, and the Indian Ocean by R. M. Burrell and Alvin J. Cottrell, September 1972 (Out of print)

Soviet Naval Power: Challenge for the 1970s by Norman Polmar, April 1972. Revised edition, September 1974

How Can We Negotiate with the Communists? by Gerald L. Steibel, March 1972 (Out of print)

Soviet Political Warfare Techniques, Espionage and Propaganda in the 1970s by Lyman B. Kirkpatrick, Jr., and Howland H. Sargeant, January 1972

The Soviet Presence in the Eastern Mediterranean by Lawrence L. Whetten, September 1971

*The Military Unbalance
Is the U.S. Becoming a Second Class Power?* June 1971 (Out of print)

The Future of South Vietnam by Brigadier F. P. Serong, February 1971 (Out of print)

Strategy and National Interests: Reflections for the Future by Bernard Brodie, January 1971 (Out of pirnt)

The Mekong River: A Challenge in Peaceful Development for Southeast Asia by Eugene R. Black, December 1970 (Out of print)

Problems of Strategy in the Pacific and Indian Oceans by George G. Thomson, October 1970

Soviet Penetration into the Middle East by Wynfred Joshua, July 1970. Revised edition, October 1971 (Out of print)

Australian Security Policies and Problems by Justus M. van der Kroef, May 1970 (Out of print)

Detente: Dilemma or Disaster? by Gerald L. Steibel, July 1969 (Out of print)

The Prudent Case for Safeguard by William R. Kintner, June 1969 (Out of print)

AGENDA PAPERS

Edited by Frank N. Trager and William Henderson
With the assistance of Dorothy E. Nicolosi

Toward A New Defense for NATO, The Case for Tactical Nuclear Weapons, July 1976

Seven Tracks to Peace in the Middle East by Frank R. Barnett, April 1975

Arms Treaties with Moscow: Unequal Terms Unevenly Applied? by Donald G. Brennan, April 1975

Toward a US Energy Policy by Klaus Knorr, March 1975

Can We Avert Economic Warfare in Raw Materials? US Agriculture as a Blue Chip by William Schneider, July 1974

OTHER PUBLICATIONS

Oil, Divestiture and National Security edited by Frank N. Trager, December 1976

Alternatives to Detente by Frank R. Barnett, July 1976

Arms, Men, and Military Budgets, Issues for Fiscal Year 1977 edited by William Schneider, Jr., and Francis P. Hoeber, May 1976

Indian Ocean Naval Limitations, Regional Issues and Global Implications by Alvin J. Cottrell and Walter F. Hahn, April 1976